INSIGHT PUBLICA®

INSIGHT PUBLICA®

Nadakkave, Kozhikode, Kerala, India
+91 4954020666 | +91 9400737475
www.insightpublica.com
e-mail: insightpublica@gmail.com
The Postmaster and Other Stories
Rabindranath Tagore
First Insight Edition: May 2020
This Edition: November 2023

ISBN 978-93-89155-99-0
Published by
InsightinPublica Printers & Publishers Pvt. Ltd.

The Postmaster and Other Stories

Rabindranath Tagore

INSIGHT PUBLICA

PREFACE

Every experienced teacher must have noticed the difficulty of instructing Indian children out of books that are specially intended for use in English schools. It is not merely that the subjects are unfamiliar, but almost every phrase has English associations that are strange to Indian ears. The environment in which they are written is unknown to the Indian school boy and his mind becomes overburdened with its details which he fails to understand. He cannot give his whole attention to the language and thus master it quickly.

The present Indian story-book avoids some at least of these impediments. The surroundings described in it are those of the students' everyday life; the sentiments and characters are familiar. The stories are simply told, and the notes at the end will be sufficient to explain obscure passages. It should be possible for the Indian student to follow the pages of the book easily and intelligently. Those students who have read the stories in the original will have the further advantage of knowing beforehand the whole trend of the narrative and thus they will be able to concentrate their thoughts on the English language itself.

It is proposed to publish together in a single volume the original stories whose English translations are given in this Reader. Versions of the same stories in the different Indian vernaculars have already appeared, and others are likely to follow.

Two of the longest stories in this book—"Master Mashai" and "The Son of Rashmani"—are reproduced in English for the first time. The rest of the stories have been taken, with slight revision, from two English volumes entitled "The Hungry Stones" and "Mashi." A short paragraph has been added from the original Bengali at the end of the story called "The Postmaster." This was unfortunately omitted in the first English edition.

The list of words to be studied has been chosen from each story in order to bring to notice different types of English words. The lists are in no sense exhaustive. The end in view has been to endeavour to create an interest in Indian words and their history, which may lead on to further study.

CONTENTS

THE POSTMASTER

The postmaster first took up his duties in the village of Ulapur. Though the village was a small one, there was an indigo factory near by, and the proprietor, an Englishman, had managed to get a post office established.

Our postmaster belonged to Calcutta. He felt like a fish out of water in this remote village. His office and living-room were in a dark thatched shed, not far from a green, slimy pond, surrounded on all sides by a dense growth.

The men employed in the indigo factory had no leisure; moreover, they were hardly desirable companions for decent folk. Nor is a Calcutta boy an adept in the art of associating with others. Among strangers he appears either proud or ill at ease. At any rate, the postmaster had but little company; nor had he much to do.

At times he tried his hand at writing a verse or two. That the movement of the leaves and the clouds of the sky were enough to fill life with joy—such were the sentiments to which he sought to give expression. But God knows that the poor fellow would have felt it as the gift of a new life, if some genie of the Arabian Nights had in one night swept away the trees, leaves and all, and replaced them with a macadamised road, hiding the clouds from view with rows of tall houses.

The postmaster's salary was small. He had to cook his own meals, which he used to share with Ratan, an orphan girl of the village, who did odd jobs for him.

When in the evening the smoke began to curl up from the village cow-sheds, and the cicalas chirped in every bush; when the mendicants of the Baül sect sang their shrill songs in their daily meeting-place, when any poet, who had attempted to watch the movement of the leaves in the dense bamboo thickets, would have felt a ghostly shiver run down his back, the postmaster would light his little lamp, and call out "Ratan."

Ratan would sit outside waiting for this call, and, instead of coming in at once, would reply, "Did you call me, sir?"

"What are you doing?" the postmaster would ask.

"I must be going to light the kitchen fire," would be the answer.

And the postmaster would say: "Oh, let the kitchen fire be for awhile; light me my pipe first."

At last Ratan would enter, with puffed-out cheeks, vigorously blowing into a flame a live coal to light the tobacco. This would give the postmaster an opportunity of conversing. "Well, Ratan," perhaps he would begin, "do you remember anything of your mother?" That was a fertile subject. Ratan partly remembered, and partly didn't. Her father had been fonder of her than her mother; him she recollected more vividly. He used to come home in the evening after his work, and one or two evenings stood out more clearly than others, like pictures in her memory. Ratan would sit on the floor near the postmaster's feet, as memories crowded in upon her. She called to mind a little brother that she had—and how on some bygone cloudy day she had played at fishing with him on the edge of the pond, with a twig for a make-believe fishing-rod. Such little incidents would drive out greater events from her mind. Thus, as they talked, it would often get very late, and the postmaster would feel too lazy to do any cooking at all. Ratan would then hastily light the fire, and toast some unleavened bread, which, with the cold remnants of the morning meal, was enough for their supper.

On some evenings, seated at his desk in the corner of the big empty shed, the postmaster too would call up memories of his own home, of his mother and his sister, of those for whom in his exile his heart was sad,—memories which were always haunting him, but which he could not talk about with the men of the factory, though he found himself naturally recalling them aloud in the presence of the simple little girl. And so it came about that the girl would allude to his people as mother, brother, and sister, as if she had known them all her life. In fact, she had a complete picture of each one of them painted in her little heart.

One noon, during a break in the rains, there was a cool soft breeze blowing; the smell of the damp grass and leaves in the hot sun felt like the warm breathing of the tired earth on one's body. A persistent bird went on all the afternoon repeating the burden of its one complaint in Nature's audience chamber.

The postmaster had nothing to do. The shimmer of the freshly washed leaves, and the banked-up remnants of the retreating rain-clouds were sights to see; and the postmaster was watching them and thinking to himself: "Oh, if only some kindred soul were near—just one loving human being whom I could hold near my heart!" This was exactly, he went on to think, what that bird was trying to say, and it was the same feeling which the murmuring leaves were striving to express. But no one knows, or would believe, that such an idea might also take possession of an ill-paid village postmaster in the deep, silent mid-day interval of his work.

The postmaster sighed, and called out "Ratan." Ratan was then sprawling beneath the guava-tree, busily engaged in eating unripe guavas. At the voice of her master, she ran up breathlessly, saying: "Were you calling me, Dada?" "I was thinking," said the postmaster, "of teaching you to read." And then for the rest of the afternoon he taught her the alphabet.

Thus, in a very short time, Ratan had got as far as the double consonants.

It seemed as though the showers of the season would never end. Canals, ditches, and hollows were all overflowing with water. Day and night the patter of rain was heard, and the croaking of frogs. The village roads became impassable, and marketing had to be done in punts.

One heavily clouded morning, the postmaster's little pupil had been long waiting outside the door for her call, but, not hearing it as usual, she took up her dog-eared book, and slowly entered the room. She found her master stretched out on his bed, and, thinking that he was resting, she was about to retire on tip-toe, when she suddenly heard her name—"Ratan!" She turned at once and asked: "Were you sleeping, Dada?" The postmaster in a plaintive voice said: "I am not well. Feel my head; is it very hot?"

In the loneliness of his exile, and in the gloom of the rains, his ailing body needed a little tender nursing. He longed to remember the touch on the forehead of soft hands with tinkling bracelets, to imagine the presence of loving womanhood, the nearness of mother and sister. And the exile was not disappointed. Ratan ceased to be a little girl. She at once stepped into the post of mother, called in the village doctor, gave the patient his pills at the proper intervals, sat up all night by his pillow, cooked his gruel for him, and every now and then asked: "Are you feeling a little better, Dada?"

It was some time before the postmaster, with weakened body, was able to leave his sick-bed. "No more of this," said he with decision. "I must get a transfer." He at once wrote off to Calcutta an application for a transfer, on the ground of the unhealthiness of the place.

Relieved from her duties as nurse, Ratan again took up her old place outside the door. But she no longer heard the same old call. She would sometimes peep inside furtively to find the postmaster sitting on his chair, or stretched on his bed, and staring absent-mindedly into the air. While Ratan was awaiting her call, the postmaster was awaiting a reply to his application. The girl read her old lessons over and over again,—her great fear was lest, when the call came, she might be found wanting in the double consonants. At last, after a week, the call did come one evening. With an overflowing heart Ratan rushed into the room with her—"Were you calling me, Dada?"

The postmaster said: "I am going away to-morrow, Ratan."

"Where are you going, Dada?"

"I am going home."

"When will you come back?"

"I am not coming back."

Ratan asked no other question. The postmaster, of his own accord, went on to tell her that his application for a transfer had been rejected, so he had resigned his post and was going home.

For a long time neither of them spoke another word. The lamp went on dimly burning, and from a leak in one corner of the thatch water dripped steadily into an earthen vessel on the floor beneath it.

After a while Ratan rose, and went off to the kitchen to prepare the meal; but she was not so quick about it as on other days. Many new things to think of had entered her little brain. When the postmaster had finished his supper, the girl suddenly asked him: "Dada, will you take me to your home?"

The postmaster laughed. "What an idea!" said he; but he did not think it necessary to explain to the girl wherein lay the absurdity.

That whole night, in her waking and in her dreams, the postmaster's laughing reply haunted her—"What an idea!"

On getting up in the morning, the postmaster found his bath ready. He had stuck to his Calcutta habit of bathing in water drawn and kept in pitchers, instead of taking a plunge in the river as was the custom of the village. For some reason or other, the girl could not ask him about the time of his departure, so she had fetched the water from the river long before sunrise, that it should be ready as early as he might want it. After the bath came a call for Ratan. She entered noiselessly, and looked silently into her master's face for orders. The master said: "You need not be anxious about my going away, Ratan; I shall tell my successor to look after you." These words were kindly meant, no doubt: but inscrutable are the ways of a woman's heart!

Ratan had borne many a scolding from her master without complaint, but these kind words she could not bear. She burst out weeping, and said: "No, no, you need not tell anybody anything at all about me; I don't want to stay on here."

The postmaster was dumbfounded. He had never seen Ratan like this before.

The new incumbent duly arrived, and the postmaster, having given over charge, prepared to depart. Just before starting he called Ratan and said: "Here is something for you; I hope it will keep you for some little time." He brought out from his pocket the whole of his month's salary, retaining only a trifle for his travelling expenses. Then Ratan fell at his feet and cried: "Oh, Dada, I pray you, don't give me anything, don't in any way trouble about me," and then she ran away out of sight.

The postmaster heaved a sigh, took up his carpet bag, put his umbrella over his shoulder, and, accompanied by a man carrying his many-coloured tin trunk, he slowly made for the boat.

When he got in and the boat was under way, and the rain-swollen river, like a stream of tears welling up from the earth, swirled and sobbed at her bows, then he felt a pain at heart; the grief-stricken face of a village girl seemed to represent for him the great unspoken pervading grief of Mother Earth herself. At one time he had an impulse to go back, and bring away along with him that lonesome waif, forsaken of the world. But the wind had just filled the sails, the boat had got well into the middle of the turbulent current, and already the village was left behind, and its outlying burning-ground came in sight.

So the traveller, borne on the breast of the swift-flowing river, consoled himself with philosophical reflections on the numberless meetings and partings going on in the world—on death, the great parting, from which none returns.

But Ratan had no philosophy. She was wandering about the post office in a flood of tears. It may be that she had still a lurking hope in some corner of her heart that her Dada would return, and that is why she could not tear herself away. Alas for our foolish human nature! Its fond mistakes are persistent. The dictates of reason take a long time to assert their own sway. The surest proofs meanwhile are disbelieved. False hope is clung to with all one's might and main, till a day comes when it has sucked the heart dry and it forcibly breaks through its bonds and departs. After that comes the misery of awakening, and then once again the longing to get back into the maze of the same mistakes.

THE CABULIWALLAH

My five years' old daughter Mini cannot live without chattering. I really believe that in all her life she has not wasted a minute in silence. Her mother is often vexed at this, and would stop her prattle, but I would not. To see Mini quiet is unnatural, and I cannot bear it long. And so my own talk with her is always lively.

One morning, for instance, when I was in the midst of the seventeenth chapter of my new novel, my little Mini stole into the room, and putting her hand into mine, said: "Father! Ramdayal the door-keeper calls a crow a krow! He doesn't know anything, does he?"

Before I could explain to her the differences of language in this world, she was embarked on the full tide of another subject. "What do you think, Father? Bhola says there is an elephant in the clouds, blowing water out of his trunk, and that is why it rains!"

And then, darting off anew, while I sat still making ready some reply to this last saying: "Father! what relation is Mother to you?"

With a grave face I contrived to say: "Go and play with Bhola, Mini! I am busy!"

The window of my room overlooks the road. The child had seated herself at my feet near my table, and was playing softly, drumming on her knees. I was hard at work on my seventeenth chapter, where Pratap Singh, the hero, had just caught Kanchanlata, the heroine, in his arms, and was about to escape with her by the third-story window of the castle, when all of a sudden Mini left her play, and ran to the window, crying: "A Cabuliwallah! a Cabuliwallah!" Sure enough in the street below was a Cabuliwallah, passing slowly along. He wore the loose, soiled clothing of his people, with a tall turban; there was a bag on his back, and he carried boxes of grapes in his hand.

I cannot tell what were my daughter's feelings at the sight of this man, but she began to call him loudly. "Ah!" I thought, "he will come in, and my seventeenth chapter will never be finished!" At which exact moment the Cabuliwallah turned, and looked up at the child. When she saw this, overcome by terror, she fled to her mother's protection and disappeared. She had a blind belief that inside the bag, which the big man carried, there were perhaps two or three other children like herself. The pedlar meanwhile entered my doorway and greeted me with a smiling face.

So precarious was the position of my hero and my heroine, that my first impulse was to stop and buy something, since the man had been called. I made some small purchases, and a conversation began about Abdurrahman, the Russians, the English, and the Frontier Policy.

As he was about to leave, he asked: "And where is the little girl, sir?"

And I, thinking that Mini must get rid of her false fear, had her brought out.

She stood by my chair, and looked at the Cabuliwallah and his bag. He offered her nuts and raisins, but she would not be tempted, and only clung the closer to me, with all her doubts increased.

This was their first meeting.

One morning, however, not many days later, as I was leaving the house, I was startled to find Mini, seated on a bench near the door, laughing and talking, with the great Cabuliwallah at her feet. In all her life, it appeared, my small daughter had never found so patient a listener, save her father. And already the corner of her little sari was stuffed with almonds and raisins, the gift of her visitor. "Why did you give her those?" I said, and taking out an eight-anna bit, I handed it to him. The man accepted the money without demur, and slipped it into his pocket.

Alas, on my return an hour later, I found the unfortunate coin had made twice its own worth of trouble! For the Cabuliwallah had given it to Mini; and her mother, catching sight of the bright round object, had pounced on the child with: "Where did you get that eight-anna bit?"

"The Cabuliwallah gave it me," said Mini cheerfully.

"The Cabuliwallah gave it you!" cried her mother much shocked. "O Mini! how could you take it from him?"

I, entering at the moment, saved her from impending disaster, and proceeded to make my own inquiries.

It was not the first or second time, I found, that the two had met. The Cabuliwallah had overcome the child's first terror by a judicious bribery of nuts and almonds, and the two were now great friends.

They had many quaint jokes, which afforded them much amusement. Seated in front of him, looking down on his gigantic frame in all her tiny dignity, Mini would ripple her face with laughter and begin: "O Cabuliwallah! Cabuliwallah! what have you got in your bag?"

And he would reply, in the nasal accents of the mountaineer: "An elephant!" Not much cause for merriment, perhaps; but how they both enjoyed the fun! And for me, this child's talk with a grown-up man had always in it something strangely fascinating.

Then the Cabuliwallah, not to be behindhand, would take his turn: "Well, little one, and when are you going to the father-in-law's house?"

Now most small Bengali maidens have heard long ago about the father-in-law's house; but we, being a little new-fangled, had kept these things from our child, and Mini at this question must have been a trifle bewildered. But she would not show it, and with ready tact replied: "Are you going there?"

Amongst men of the Cabuliwallah's class, however, it is well known that the words father-in-law's house have a double meaning. It is a euphemism for jail, the place where we are well cared for, at no expense to ourselves. In this sense would the sturdy pedlar take my daughter's question. "Ah," he would say, shaking his fist at an invisible policeman, "I will thrash my father-in-law!" Hearing this, and picturing the poor discomfited relative, Mini would go off into peals of laughter, in which her formidable friend would join.

These were autumn mornings, the very time of year when kings of old went forth to conquest; and I, never stirring from my little corner in Calcutta, would let my mind wander over the whole world. At the very name of another country, my heart would go out to it, and at the sight of a foreigner in the streets, I would fall to weaving a network of dreams,—the mountains, the glens, and the forests of his distant home, with his cottage in its setting, and the free and independent life of far-away wilds. Perhaps the scenes of travel conjure themselves up before me and pass and repass in my imagination all the more vividly, because I lead such a vegetable existence that a call to travel would fall upon me like a thunder-bolt. In the presence of this Cabuliwallah I was immediately transported to the foot of arid mountain peaks, with narrow little defiles twisting in and out amongst their towering heights. I could see the string of camels bearing the merchandise, and the company of turbanned merchants carrying some their queer old firearms, and some their spears, journeying downward towards the plains. I could see—. But at some such point Mini's mother would intervene, imploring me to "beware of that man."

Mini's mother is unfortunately a very timid lady. Whenever she hears a noise in the street, or sees people coming towards the house, she always jumps to the conclusion that they are either thieves, or drunkards, or snakes, or tigers, or malaria, or cockroaches, or caterpillars. Even after all these years of experience, she is not able to overcome her terror. So she was full of doubts about the Cabuliwallah, and used to beg me to keep a watchful eye on him.

I tried to laugh her fear gently away, but then she would turn round on me seriously, and ask me solemn questions:—

Were children never kidnapped?

Was it, then, not true that there was slavery in Cabul?

Was it so very absurd that this big man should be able to carry off a tiny child?

I urged that, though not impossible, it was highly improbable. But this was not enough, and her dread persisted. As it was indefinite, however, it did not seem right to forbid the man the house, and the intimacy went on unchecked.

Once a year in the middle of January Rahmun, the Cabuliwallah, was in the habit of returning to his country, and as the time approached he would be very busy, going from house to house collecting his debts. This year, however, he could always find time to come and see Mini. It would have seemed to an outsider that there was some conspiracy between the two, for when he could not come in the morning, he would appear in the evening.

Even to me it was a little startling now and then, in the corner of a dark room, suddenly to surprise this tall, loose-garmented, much bebagged man; but when Mini would run in smiling, with her "O Cabuliwallah! Cabuliwallah!" and the two friends, so far apart in age, would subside into their old laughter and their old jokes, I felt reassured.

One morning, a few days before he had made up his mind to go, I was correcting my proof sheets in my study. It was chilly weather. Through the window the rays of the sun touched my feet, and the slight warmth was very welcome. It was almost eight o'clock, and the early pedestrians were returning home with their heads covered. All at once I heard an uproar in the street, and, looking out, saw Rahmun being led away bound between two policemen, and behind them a crowd of curious boys. There were blood-stains on the clothes of the Cabuliwallah, and one of the policemen carried a knife. Hurrying out, I stopped them, and inquired what it all meant. Partly from one, partly from another, I gathered that a certain neighbour had owed the pedlar something for a Rampuri shawl, but had falsely denied having bought it, and that in the course of the quarrel Rahmun had struck him. Now, in the heat of his excitement, the prisoner began calling his enemy all sorts of names, when suddenly in a verandah of my house appeared my little Mini, with her usual exclamation: "O Cabuliwallah! Cabuliwallah!" Rahmun's face lighted up as he turned to her. He had no bag under his arm to-day, so she could not discuss the elephant with him. She at once therefore proceeded to the next question: "Are you going to the father-in-law's house?" Rahmun laughed and said: "Just where I am going, little one!" Then, seeing that the reply did not amuse the child, he held up his fettered hands. "Ah!" he said, "I would have thrashed that old father-in-law, but my hands are bound!"

On a charge of murderous assault, Rahmun was sentenced to some years' imprisonment.

Time passed away and he was not remembered. The accustomed work in the accustomed place was ours, and the thought of the once free mountaineer spending his years in prison seldom or never occurred to us. Even my light-hearted Mini, I am ashamed to say, forgot her old friend. New companions filled her life. As she grew older, she spent more of her time with girls. So much time indeed did she spend with them that she came no more, as she used to do, to her father's room. I was scarcely on speaking terms with her.

Years had passed away. It was once more autumn and we had made arrangements for our Mini's marriage. It was to take place during the Puja Holidays. With Durga returning to Kailas, the light of our home also was to depart to her husband's house, and leave her father's in the shadow.

The morning was bright. After the rains, there was a sense of ablution in the air, and the sun-rays looked like pure gold. So bright were they, that they gave a beautiful radiance even to the sordid brick walls of our Calcutta lanes. Since early dawn that day the wedding-pipes had been sounding, and at each beat my own heart throbbed. The wail of the tune, Bhairavi, seemed to intensify my pain at the approaching separation. My Mini was to be married that night.

From early morning noise and bustle had pervaded the house. In the courtyard the canopy had to be slung on its bamboo poles; the chandeliers with their tinkling sound must be hung in each room and verandah. There was no end of hurry and excitement. I was sitting in my study, looking through the accounts, when some one entered, saluting respectfully, and stood before me. It was Rahmun the Cabuliwallah. At first I did not recognise him. He had no bag, nor the long hair, nor the same vigour that he used to have. But he smiled, and I knew him again.

"When did you come, Rahmun?" I asked him.

"Last evening," he said, "I was released from jail."

The words struck harsh upon my ears. I had never before talked with one who had wounded his fellow, and my heart shrank within itself when I realised this; for I felt that the day would have been better-omened had he not turned up.

"There are ceremonies going on," I said, "and I am busy. Could you perhaps come another day?"

At once he turned to go; but as he reached the door he hesitated, and said: "May I not see the little one, sir, for a moment?" It was his belief that Mini was still the same. He had pictured her running to him as she used, calling "O Cabuliwallah! Cabuliwallah!" He had imagined too that they would laugh and talk together, just as of old. In fact, in memory of former days he had brought, carefully wrapped up in paper, a few almonds and raisins and grapes, obtained somehow from a countryman; for his own little fund was dispersed.

I said again: "There is a ceremony in the house, and you will not be able to see any one to-day."

The man's face fell. He looked wistfully at me for a moment, then said "Good morning," and went out.

I felt a little sorry, and would have called him back, but I found he was returning of his own accord. He came close up to me holding out his offerings with the words: "I brought these few things, sir, for the little one. Will you give them to her?"

I took them and was going to pay him, but he caught my hand and said: "You are very kind, sir! Keep me in your recollection. Do not offer me money!—You have a little girl: I too have one like her in my own home. I think of her, and bring fruits to your child—not to make a profit for myself."

Saying this, he put his hand inside his big loose robe, and brought out a small and dirty piece of paper. With great care he unfolded this, and smoothed it out with both hands on my table. It bore the impression of a little hand. Not a photograph. Not a drawing. The impression of an ink-smeared hand laid flat on the paper. This touch of his own little daughter had been always on his heart, as he had come year after year to Calcutta to sell his wares in the streets.

Tears came to my eyes. I forgot that he was a poor Cabuli fruit-seller, while I was—. But no, what was I more than he? He also was a father.

That impression of the hand of his little Pārbati in her distant mountain home reminded me of my own little Mini.

I sent for Mini immediately from the inner apartment. Many difficulties were raised, but I would not listen. Clad in the red silk of her wedding-day, with the sandal paste on her forehead, and adorned as a young bride, Mini came, and stood bashfully before me.

The Cabuliwallah looked a little staggered at the apparition. He could not revive their old friendship. At last he smiled and said: "Little one, are you going to your father-in-law's house?"

But Mini now understood the meaning of the word "father-in-law," and she could not reply to him as of old. She flushed up at the question, and stood before him with her bride-like face turned down.

I remembered the day when the Cabuliwallah and my Mini had first met, and I felt sad. When she had gone, Rahmun heaved a deep sigh, and sat down on the floor. The idea had suddenly come to him that his daughter too must have grown in this long time, and that he would have to make friends with her anew. Assuredly he would not find her as he used to know her. And besides, what might not have happened to her in these eight years?

The marriage-pipes sounded, and the mild autumn sun streamed round us. But Rahmun sat in the little Calcutta lane, and saw before him the barren mountains of Afghanistan.

I took out a bank-note and gave it to him, saying: "Go back to your own daughter, Rahmun, in your own country, and may the happiness of your meeting bring good fortune to my child!"

Having made this present, I had to curtail some of the festivities. I could not have the electric lights I had intended, nor the military band, and the ladies of the house were despondent at it. But to me the wedding-feast was all the brighter for the thought that in a distant land a long-lost father met again with his only child.

THE HOME-COMING

Phatik Chakravorti was ringleader among the boys of the village. A new mischief got into his head. There was a heavy log lying on the mud-flat of the river waiting to be shaped into a mast for a boat. He decided that they should all work together to shift the log by main force from its place and roll it away. The owner of the log would be angry and surprised, and they would all enjoy the fun. Every one seconded the proposal, and it was carried unanimously.

But just as the fun was about to begin, Mākhan, Phatik's younger brother, sauntered up and sat down on the log in front of them all without a word. The boys were puzzled for a moment. He was pushed, rather timidly, by one of the boys and told to get up; but he remained quite unconcerned. He appeared like a young philosopher meditating on the futility of games. Phatik was furious. "Mākhan," he cried, "if you don't get down this minute I'll thrash you!"

Mākhan only moved to a more comfortable position.

Now, if Phatik was to keep his regal dignity before the public, it was clear he ought to carry out his threat. But his courage failed him at the crisis. His fertile brain, however, rapidly seized upon a new manœuvre which would discomfit his brother and afford his followers an added amusement. He gave the word of command to roll the log and Mākhan over together. Mākhan heard the order and made it a point of honour to stick on. But he overlooked the fact, like those who attempt earthly fame in other matters, that there was peril in it.

The boys began to heave at the log with all their might, calling out, "One, two, three, go!" At the word "go" the log went; and with it went Mākhan's philosophy, glory and all.

The other boys shouted themselves hoarse with delight. But Phatik was a little frightened. He knew what was coming. And, sure enough, Mākhan rose from Mother Earth blind as Fate and screaming like the Furies. He rushed at

Phatik and scratched his face and beat him and kicked him, and then went crying home. The first act of the drama was over.

Phatik wiped his face, and sat down on the edge of a sunken barge by the river bank, and began to chew a piece of grass. A boat came up to the landing and a middle-aged man, with grey hair and dark moustache, stepped on shore. He saw the boy sitting there doing nothing and asked him where the Chakravortis lived. Phatik went on chewing the grass and said: "Over there," but it was quite impossible to tell where he pointed. The stranger asked him again. He swung his legs to and fro on the side of the barge and said: "Go and find out," and continued to chew the grass as before.

But now a servant came down from the house and told Phatik his mother wanted him. Phatik refused to move. But the servant was the master on this occasion. He took Phatik up roughly and carried him, kicking and struggling in impotent rage.

When Phatik came into the house, his mother saw him. She called out angrily: "So you have been hitting Mākhan again?"

Phatik answered indignantly: "No, I haven't! Who told you that?"

His mother shouted: "Don't tell lies! You have."

Phatik said sullenly: "I tell you, I haven't. You ask Mākhan!" But Mākhan thought it best to stick to his previous statement. He said: "Yes, mother. Phatik did hit me."

Phatik's patience was already exhausted. He could not bear this injustice. He rushed at Mākhan and hammered him with blows: "Take that," he cried, "and that, and that, for telling lies."

His mother took Mākhan's side in a moment, and pulled Phatik away, beating him with her hands. When Phatik pushed her aside, she shouted out: "What! you little villain! Would you hit your own mother?"

It was just at this critical juncture that the grey-haired stranger arrived. He asked what was the matter. Phatik looked sheepish and ashamed.

But when his mother stepped back and looked at the stranger, her anger was changed to surprise. For she recognized her brother and cried: "Why, Dada! Where have you come from?"

As she said these words, she bowed to the ground and touched his feet. Her brother had gone away soon after she had married; and he had started business in Bombay. His sister had lost her husband while he was there. Bishamber had now come back to Calcutta and had at once made enquiries about his sister. He had then hastened to see her as soon as he found out where she was.

The next few days were full of rejoicing. The brother asked after the education of the two boys. He was told by his sister that Phatik was a perpetual nuisance. He was lazy, disobedient, and wild. But Mākhan was as good as gold, as quiet as a lamb, and very fond of reading. Bishamber kindly offered to take Phatik off his sister's hands and educate him with his own children in Calcutta. The widowed mother readily agreed. When his uncle asked Phatik if he would like to go to Calcutta with him, his joy knew no bounds and he said: "Oh, yes, uncle!" in a way that made it quite clear that he meant it.

It was an immense relief to the mother to get rid of Phatik. She had a prejudice against the boy, and no love was lost between the two brothers. She was in daily fear that he would either drown Mākhan some day in the river, or break his head in a fight, or run him into some danger. At the same time she was a little distressed to see Phatik's extreme eagerness to get away.

Phatik, as soon as all was settled, kept asking his uncle every minute when they were to start. He was on pins and needles all day long with excitement and lay awake most of the night. He bequeathed to Mākhan, in perpetuity, his fishing-rod, his big kite, and his marbles. Indeed, at this time of departure, his generosity towards Mākhan was unbounded.

When they reached Calcutta, Phatik made the acquaintance of his aunt for the first time. She was by no means pleased with this unnecessary addition to her family. She found her own three boys quite enough to manage without taking any one else. And to bring a village lad of fourteen into their midst was terribly upsetting. Bishamber should really have thought twice before committing such an indiscretion.

In this world of human affairs there is no worse nuisance than a boy at the age of fourteen. He is neither ornamental nor useful. It is impossible to shower affection on him as on a little boy; and he is always getting in the way. If he talks with a childish lisp he is called a baby, and if he answers in a grown-up way he is called impertinent. In fact any talk at all from him is resented. Then he is at the unattractive, growing age. He grows out of his clothes with indecent haste; his voice grows hoarse and breaks and quavers; his face grows suddenly angular and unsightly. It is easy to excuse the shortcomings of early childhood, but it is hard to tolerate even unavoidable lapses in a boy of fourteen. The lad himself becomes painfully self-conscious. When he talks with elderly people he is either unduly forward, or else so unduly shy that he appears ashamed of his very existence.

Yet it is at this very age when, in his heart of hearts, a young lad most craves for recognition and love; and he becomes the devoted slave of any one who shows him consideration. But none dare openly love him, for that would be regarded as undue indulgence and therefore bad for the boy. So, what with scolding and chiding, he becomes very much like a stray dog that has lost his master.

For a boy of fourteen his own home is the only Paradise. To live in a strange house with strange people is little short of torture, while the height of bliss is to receive the kind looks of women and never to be slighted by them.

It was anguish to Phatik to be the unwelcome guest in his aunt's house, despised by this elderly woman and slighted on every occasion. If ever she asked him to do anything for her, he would be so overjoyed that he would overdo it; and then she would tell him not to be so stupid, but to get on with his lessons.

The cramped atmosphere of neglect oppressed Phatik so much that he felt that he could hardly breathe. He wanted to go out into the open country and fill his lungs with fresh air. But there was no open country to go to. Surrounded on all sides by Calcutta houses and walls, he would dream night after night of his village home and long to be back there. He remembered the glorious meadow where he used to fly his kite all day long; the broad river-banks where he would wander about the live-long day singing and shouting for joy; the narrow brook where he could go and dive and swim at any time he liked. He thought of his band of boy companions over whom he was despot; and, above all, the memory of that tyrant mother of his, who had such a prejudice against him, occupied him day and night. A kind of physical love like that of animals, a longing to be in the presence of the one who is loved, an inexpressible wistfulness during absence, a silent cry of the inmost heart for the mother, like the lowing of a calf in the twilight,—this love, which was almost an animal instinct, agitated the shy, nervous, lean, uncouth and ugly boy. No one could understand it, but it preyed upon his mind continually.

There was no more backward boy in the whole school than Phatik. He gaped and remained silent when the teacher asked him a question, and like an overladen ass patiently suffered all the blows that came down on his back. When other boys were out at play, he stood wistfully by the window and gazed at the roofs of the distant houses. And if by chance he espied children playing on the open terrace of any roof, his heart would ache with longing.

One day he summoned up all his courage and asked his uncle: "Uncle, when can I go home?"

His uncle answered: "Wait till the holidays come."

But the holidays would not come till October and there was a long time still to wait.

One day Phatik lost his lesson book. Even with the help of books he had found it very difficult indeed to prepare his lesson. Now it was impossible. Day after day the teacher would cane him unmercifully. His condition became so abjectly miserable that even his cousins were ashamed to own him. They began to jeer and insult him more than the other boys. He went to his aunt at last and told her that he had lost his book.

His aunt pursed her lips in contempt and said: "You great clumsy, country lout! How can I afford, with all my family, to buy you new books five times a month?"

That night, on his way back from school, Phatik had a bad headache with a fit of shivering. He felt he was going to have an attack of malarial fever. His one great fear was that he would be a nuisance to his aunt.

The next morning Phatik was nowhere to be seen. All searches in the neighbourhood proved futile. The rain had been pouring in torrents all night, and those who went out in search of the boy got drenched through to the skin. At last Bishamber asked help from the police.

At the end of the day a police van stopped at the door before the house. It was still raining and the streets were all flooded. Two constables brought out Phatik in their arms and placed him before Bishamber. He was wet through from head to foot, muddy all over, his face and eyes flushed red with fever and his limbs trembling. Bishamber carried him in his arms and took him into the inner apartments. When his wife saw him she exclaimed: "What a heap of trouble this boy has given us! Hadn't you better send him home?"

Phatik heard her words and sobbed out loud: "Uncle, I was just going home; but they dragged me back again."

The fever rose very high, and all that night the boy was delirious. Bishamber brought in a doctor. Phatik opened his eyes, flushed with fever, and looked up to the ceiling and said vacantly: "Uncle, have the holidays come yet?"

Bishamber wiped the tears from his own eyes and took Phatik's lean and burning hands in his own and sat by him through the night. The boy began again to mutter. At last his voice became excited: "Mother!" he cried, "don't beat me like that.... Mother! I am telling the truth!"

The next day Phatik became conscious for a short time. He turned his eyes about the room, as if expecting some one to come. At last, with an air of disappointment, his head sank back on the pillow. He turned his face to the wall with a deep sigh.

Bishamber knew his thoughts and bending down his head whispered: "Phatik, I have sent for your mother."

The day went by. The doctor said in a troubled voice that the boy's condition was very critical.

Phatik began to cry out: "By the mark—three fathoms. By the mark—four fathoms. By the mark——." He had heard the sailor on the river-steamer calling out the mark on the plumb-line. Now he was himself plumbing an unfathomable sea.

Later in the day Phatik's mother burst into the room, like a whirlwind, and began to toss from side to side and moan and cry in a loud voice.

Bishamber tried to calm her agitation, but she flung herself on the bed, and cried: "Phatik, my darling, my darling."

Phatik stopped his restless movements for a moment. His hands ceased beating up and down. He said: "Eh?"

The mother cried again: "Phatik, my darling, my darling."

Phatik very slowly turned his head and without seeing anybody said: "Mother, the holidays have come."

ONCE THERE WAS A KING

"Once upon a time there was a king."

When we were children there was no need to know who the king in the fairy story was. It didn't matter whether he was called Shiladitya or Shaliban, whether he lived at Kashi or Kanauj. The thing that made a seven-year-old boy's heart go thump, thump with delight was this one sovereign truth, this reality of all realities: "Once there was a king."

But the readers of this modern age are far more exact and exacting. When they hear such an opening to a story, they are at once critical and suspicious. They apply the searchlight of science to its legendary haze and ask: "Which king?"

The story-tellers have become more precise in their turn. They are no longer content with the old indefinite, "There was a king," but assume instead a look of profound learning and begin: "Once there was a king named Ajatasatru."

The modern reader's curiosity, however, is not so easily satisfied. He blinks at the author through his scientific spectacles and asks again: "Which Ajatasatru?"

When we were young, we understood all sweet things; and we could detect the sweets of a fairy story by an unerring science of our own. We never cared for such useless things as knowledge. We only cared for truth. And our unsophisticated little hearts knew well where the Crystal Palace of Truth lay and how to reach it. But to-day we are expected to write pages of facts, while the truth is simply this:

"There was a king."

I remember vividly that evening in Calcutta when the fairy story began. The rain and the storm had been incessant. The whole of the city was flooded.

The water was knee-deep in our lane. I had a straining hope, which was almost a certainty, that my tutor would be prevented from coming that evening. I sat on the stool in the far corner of the verandah looking down the lane, with a heart beating faster and faster. Every minute I kept my eye on the rain, and when it began to diminish I prayed with all my might: "Please, God, send some more rain till half-past seven is over." For I was quite ready to believe that there was no other need for rain except to protect one helpless boy one evening in one corner of Calcutta from the deadly clutches of his tutor.

If not in answer to my prayer, at any rate according to some grosser law of nature, the rain did not give up.

But, alas, nor did my teacher!

Exactly to the minute, in the bend of the lane, I saw his approaching umbrella. The great bubble of hope burst in my breast, and my heart collapsed. Truly, if there is a punishment to fit the crime after death, then my tutor will be born again as me, and I shall be born as my tutor.

As soon as I saw his umbrella I ran as hard as I could to my mother's room. My mother and my grandmother were sitting opposite one another playing cards by the light of a lamp. I ran into the room, and flung myself on the bed beside my mother, and said:

"Mother, the tutor has come, and I have such a bad headache; couldn't I have no lessons to-day?"

I hope no child of immature age will be allowed to read this story, and I sincerely trust it will not be used in text-books or primers for junior classes. For what I did was dreadfully bad, and I received no punishment whatever. On the contrary, my wickedness was crowned with success.

My mother said to me: "All right," and turning to the servant added: "Tell the tutor that he can go back home."

It was perfectly plain that she didn't think my illness very serious, as she went on with her game as before and took no further notice. And I also, burying my head in the pillow, laughed to my heart's content. We perfectly understood one another, my mother and I.

But every one must know how hard it is for a boy of seven years old to keep up the illusion of illness for a long time. After about a minute I got hold of Grandmother and said: "Grannie, do tell me a story."

I had to ask this many times. Grannie and Mother went on playing cards and took no notice. At last Mother said to me: "Child, don't bother. Wait till we've finished our game." But I persisted: "Grannie, do tell me a story." I told Mother she could finish her game to-morrow, but she must let Grannie tell me a story there and then.

At last Mother threw down the cards and said: "You had better do what he wants. I can't manage him." Perhaps she had it in her mind that she would have no tiresome tutor on the morrow, while I should be obliged to be back at those stupid lessons.

As soon as ever Mother had given way, I rushed at Grannie. I got hold of her hand, and, dancing with delight, dragged her inside my mosquito curtain on to the bed. I clutched hold of the bolster with both hands in my excitement, and jumped up and down with joy, and when I had got a little quieter said: "Now, Grannie, let's have the story!"

Grannie went on: "And the king had a queen."

That was good to begin with. He had only one!

It is usual for kings in fairy stories to be extravagant in queens. And whenever we hear that there are two queens our hearts begin to sink. One is sure to be unhappy. But in Grannie's story that danger was past. He had only one queen.

We next hear that the king had not got any son. At the age of seven I didn't think there was any need to bother if a man had no son. He might only have been in the way.

Nor are we greatly excited when we hear that the king has gone away into the forest to practise austerities in order to get a son. There was only one thing that would have made me go into the forest, and that was to get away from my tutor!

But the king left behind with his queen a small girl, who grew up into a beautiful princess.

Twelve years pass away, and the king goes on practising austerities, and never thinks all this while of his beautiful daughter. The princess has reached the full bloom of her youth. The age of marriage has passed, but the king does not return. And the queen pines away with grief and cries: "Is my golden daughter destined to die unmarried? Ah me, what a fate is mine!"

Then the queen sent men to the king to entreat him earnestly to come back for a single night and take one meal in the palace. And the king consented.

The queen cooked with her own hand, and with the greatest care, sixty-four dishes. She made a seat for him of sandal-wood and arranged the food in plates of gold and cups of silver. The princess stood behind with the peacock-tail fan in her hand. The king, after twelve years' absence, came into the house, and the princess waved the fan, lighting up all the room with her beauty. The king looked in his daughter's face and forgot to take his food.

At last he asked his queen: "Pray, who is this girl whose beauty shines as the gold image of the goddess? Whose daughter is she?"

The queen beat her forehead and cried: "Ah, how evil is my fate! Do you not know your own daughter?"

The king was struck with amazement. He said at last: "My tiny daughter has grown to be a woman."

"What else?" the queen said with a sigh. "Do you not know that twelve years have passed by?"

"But why did you not give her in marriage?" asked the king.

"You were away," the queen said. "And how could I find her a suitable husband?"

The king became vehement with excitement. "The first man I see to-morrow," he said, "when I come out of the palace shall marry her."

The princess went on waving her fan of peacock feathers, and the king finished his meal.

The next morning, as the king came out of his palace, he saw the son of a Brahman gathering sticks in the forest outside the palace gates. His age was about seven or eight.

The King said: "I will marry my daughter to him."

Who can interfere with a king's command? At once the boy was called, and the marriage garlands were exchanged between him and the princess.

At this point I came up close to my wise Grannie and asked her eagerly: "When then?"

In the bottom of my heart there was a devout wish to substitute myself for that fortunate wood-gatherer of seven years old. The night was resonant with the patter of rain. The earthen lamp by my bedside was burning low. My grandmother's voice droned on as she told the story. And all these things served to create in a corner of my credulous heart the belief that I had been gathering sticks in the dawn of some indefinite time in the kingdom of some unknown king, and in a moment garlands had been exchanged between me and the princess, beautiful as the Goddess of Grace. She had a gold band on her hair and gold earrings in her ears. She had a necklace and bracelets of gold, and a golden waist-chain round her waist, and a pair of golden anklets tinkled above her feet.

If my grandmother were an author, how many explanations she would have to offer for this little story! First of all, every one would ask why the king remained twelve years in the forest? Secondly, why should the king's daughter remain unmarried all that while? This would be regarded as absurd.

Even if she could have got so far without a quarrel, still there would have been a great hue and cry about the marriage itself. First, it never happened. Secondly, how could there be a marriage between a princess of the Warrior Caste and a boy of the priestly Brahman Caste? Her readers would have imagined at once that the writer was preaching against our social customs in an underhand way. And they would write letters to the papers.

So I pray with all my heart that my grandmother may be born a grandmother again, and not through some cursed fate take birth as her luckless grandson.

With a throb of joy and delight, I asked Grannie: "What then?"

Grannie went on: Then the princess took her little husband away in great distress, and built a large palace with seven wings, and began to cherish her husband with great care.

I jumped up and down in my bed and clutched at the bolster more tightly than ever and said: "What then?"

Grannie continued: The little boy went to school and learnt many lessons from his teachers, and as he grew up his class-fellows began to ask him: "Who is that beautiful lady living with you in the palace with the seven wings?"

The Brahman's son was eager to know who she was. He could only remember how one day he had been gathering sticks and a great disturbance arose. But all that was so long ago that he had no clear recollection.

Four or five years passed in this way. His companions always asked him: "Who is that beautiful lady in the palace with the seven wings?" And the Brahman's son would come back from school and sadly tell the princess: "My school companions always ask me who is that beautiful lady in the palace with the seven wings, and I can give them no reply. Tell me, oh, tell me, who you are!"

The princess said: "Let it pass to-day. I will tell you some other day." And every day the Brahman's son would ask: "Who are you?" and the princess would reply: "Let it pass to-day. I will tell you some other day." In this manner four or five more years passed away.

At last the Brahman's son became very impatient and said: "If you do not tell me to-day who you are, O beautiful lady, I will leave this palace with the seven wings." Then the princess said: "I will certainly tell you to-morrow."

Next day the Brahman's son, as soon as he came home from school, said: "Now, tell me who you are." The princess said: "To-night I will tell you after supper, when you are in bed."

The Brahman's son said: "Very well"; and he began to count the hours in expectation of the night. And the princess, on her side, spread white flowers over the golden bed, and lighted a gold lamp with fragrant oil, and adorned her hair, and dressed herself in a beautiful robe of blue, and began to count the hours in expectation of the night.

That evening when her husband, the Brahman's son, had finished his meal, too excited almost to eat, and had gone to the golden bed in the bedchamber strewn with flowers, he said to himself: "To-night I shall surely know who this beautiful lady is in the palace with the seven wings."

The princess took for her food that which was left over by her husband, and slowly entered the bedchamber. She had to answer that night the question, who was the beautiful lady that lived in the palace with the seven wings. And as she went up to the bed to tell him she found a serpent had crept out of the flowers and had bitten the Brahman's son. Her boy-husband was lying on the bed of flowers, with face pale in death.

My heart suddenly ceased to throb, and I asked with choking voice: "What then?"

Grannie said: "Then ..."

But what is the use of going on any further with the story? It would only lead on to what was more and more impossible. The boy of seven did not know that, if there were some "What then?" after death, no grandmother of a grandmother could tell us all about it.

But the child's faith never admits defeat, and it would snatch at the mantle of death itself to turn him back. It would be outrageous for him to think that such a story of one teacherless evening could so suddenly come to a stop. Therefore the grandmother had to call back her story from the ever-shut chamber of the great End, but she does it so simply: it is merely by floating the dead body on a banana stem on the river, and having some incantations read by a magician. But in that rainy night and in the dim light of a lamp death loses all its horror in the mind of the boy, and seems nothing more than a deep slumber of a single night. When the story ends the tired eyelids are weighed down with sleep. Thus it is that we send the little body of the child floating on the back of sleep over the still water of time, and then in the morning read a few verses of incantation to restore him to the world of life and light.

THE CHILD'S RETURN

I

Raicharan was twelve years old when he came as a servant to his master's house. He belonged to the same caste as his master and was given his master's little son to nurse. As time went on the boy left Raicharan's arms to go to school. From school he went on to college, and after college he entered the judicial service. Always, until he married, Raicharan was his sole attendant.

But when a mistress came into the house, Raicharan found two masters instead of one. All his former influence passed to the new mistress. This was compensated by a fresh arrival. Anukul had a son born to him and Raicharan by his unsparing attentions soon got a complete hold over the child. He used to toss him up in his arms, call to him in absurd baby language, put his face close to the baby's and draw it away again with a laugh.

Presently the child was able to crawl and cross the doorway. When Raicharan went to catch him, he would scream with mischievous laughter and make for safety. Raicharan was amazed at the profound skill and exact judgment the baby showed when pursued. He would say to his mistress with a look of awe and mystery: "Your son will be a judge some day."

New wonders came in their turn. When the baby began to toddle, that was to Raicharan an epoch in human history. When he called his father Ba-ba and his mother Ma-ma and Raicharan Chan-na, then Raicharan's ecstasy knew no bounds. He went out to tell the news to all the world.

After a while Raicharan was asked to show his ingenuity in other ways. He had, for instance, to play the part of a horse, holding the reins between his teeth and prancing with his feet. He had also to wrestle with his little charge; and if he could not, by a wrestler's trick, fall on his back defeated at the end a great outcry was certain.

About this time Anukul was transferred to a district on the banks of the Padma. On his way through Calcutta he bought his son a little go-cart. He bought him also a yellow satin waistcoat, a gold-laced cap, and some gold bracelets and anklets. Raicharan was wont to take these out and put them on his little charge, with ceremonial pride, whenever they went for a walk.

Then came the rainy season and day after day the rain poured down in torrents. The hungry river, like an enormous serpent, swallowed down terraces, villages, cornfields, and covered with its flood the tall grasses and wild casuarinas on the sandbanks. From time to time there was a deep thud as the river-banks crumbled. The unceasing roar of the main current could be heard from far away. Masses of foam, carried swiftly past, proved to the eye the swiftness of the stream.

One afternoon the rain cleared. It was cloudy, but cool and bright. Raicharan's little despot did not want to stay in on such a fine afternoon. His lordship climbed into the go-cart. Raicharan, between the shafts, dragged him slowly along till he reached the rice-fields on the banks of the river. There was no one in the fields and no boat on the stream. Across the water, on the farther side, the clouds were rifted in the west. The silent ceremonial of the setting sun was revealed in all its glowing splendour. In the midst of that stillness the child, all of a sudden, pointed with his finger in front of him and cried: "Chan-na! Pitty fow."

Close by on a mud-flat stood a large Kadamba tree in full flower. My lord, the baby, looked at it with greedy eyes and Raicharan knew his meaning. Only a short time before he had made, out of these very flower balls, a small go-cart; and the child had been so entirely happy dragging it about with a string, that for the whole day Raicharan was not asked to put on the reins at all. He was promoted from a horse into a groom.

But Raicharan had no wish that evening to go splashing knee-deep through the mud to reach the flowers. So he quickly pointed his finger in the opposite direction, calling out: "Look, baby, look! Look at the bird." And with all sorts of curious noises he pushed the go-cart rapidly away from the tree.

But a child, destined to be a judge, cannot be put off so easily. And besides, there was at the time nothing to attract his eyes. And you cannot keep up for ever the pretence of an imaginary bird.

The little Master's mind was made up, and Raicharan was at his wits' end. "Very well, baby," he said at last, "you sit still in the cart, and I'll go and get you the pretty flower. Only mind you don't go near the water."

As he said this, he made his legs bare to the knee, and waded through the oozing mud towards the tree.

The moment Raicharan had gone, his little Master's thoughts went off at racing speed to the forbidden water. The baby saw the river rushing by, splashing and gurgling as it went. It seemed as though the disobedient wavelets themselves were running away from some greater Raicharan with the laughter of a thousand children. At the sight of their mischief, the heart of the human child grew excited and restless. He got down stealthily from the go-cart and toddled off towards the river. On his way he picked up a small stick and leant over the bank of the stream pretending to fish. The mischievous fairies of the river with their mysterious voices seemed inviting him into their play-house.

Raicharan had plucked a handful of flowers from the tree and was carrying them back in the end of his cloth, with his face wreathed in smiles. But when he reached the go-cart there was no one there. He looked on all sides and there was no one there. He looked back at the cart and there was no one there.

In that first terrible moment his blood froze within him. Before his eyes the whole universe swam round like a dark mist. From the depth of his broken heart he gave one piercing cry: "Master, Master, little Master."

But no voice answered "Chan-na." No child laughed mischievously back: no scream of baby delight welcomed his return. Only the river ran on with its splashing, gurgling noise as before,—as though it knew nothing at all and had no time to attend to such a tiny human event as the death of a child.

As the evening passed by Raicharan's mistress became very anxious. She sent men out on all sides to search. They went with lanterns in their hands and reached at last the banks of the Padma. There they found Raicharan rushing up and down the fields, like a stormy wind, shouting the cry of despair: "Master, Master, little Master!"

When they got Raicharan home at last, he fell prostrate at the feet of his mistress. They shook him, and questioned him, and asked him repeatedly where he had left the child; but all he could say was that he knew nothing.

Though every one held the opinion that the Padma had swallowed the child, there was a lurking doubt left in the mind. For a band of gipsies had been noticed outside the village that afternoon, and some suspicion rested on them. The mother went so far in her wild grief as to think it possible that Raicharan himself had stolen the child. She called him aside with piteous entreaty and said: "Raicharan, give me back my baby. Give me back my child. Take from me any money you ask, but give me back my child!"

Raicharan only beat his forehead in reply. His mistress ordered him out of the house.

Anukul tried to reason his wife out of this wholly unjust suspicion: "Why on earth," he said, "should he commit such a crime as that?"

The mother only replied: "The baby had gold ornaments on his body. Who knows?"

It was impossible to reason with her after that.

II

Raicharan went back to his own village. Up to this time he had had no son, and there was no hope that any child would now be born to him. But it came about before the end of a year that his wife gave birth to a son and died.

An overwhelming resentment at first grew up in Raicharan's heart at the sight of this new baby. At the back of his mind was resentful suspicion that it had come as a usurper in place of the little Master. He also thought it would be a grave offence to be happy with a son of his own after what had happened to his master's little child. Indeed, if it had not been for a widowed sister, who mothered the new baby, it would not have lived long.

But a change gradually came over Raicharan's mind. A wonderful thing happened. This new baby in turn began to crawl about, and cross the doorway with mischief in its face. It also showed an amusing cleverness in making its escape to safety. Its voice, its sounds of laughter and tears, its gestures, were those of the little Master. On some days, when Raicharan listened to its crying, his heart suddenly began thumping wildly against his ribs, and it seemed to him that his former little Master was crying somewhere in the unknown land of death because he had lost his Chan-na.

Phailna (for that was the name Raicharan's sister gave to the new baby) soon began to talk. It learnt to say Ba-ba and Ma-ma with a baby accent. When Raicharan heard those familiar sounds the mystery suddenly became clear. The little Master could not cast off the spell of his Chan-na and therefore he had been reborn in his own house.

The three arguments in favour of this were, to Raicharan, altogether beyond dispute:

The new baby was born soon after his little master's death.

His wife could never have accumulated such merit as to give birth to a son in middle age.

The new baby walked with a toddle and called out Ba-ba and Ma-ma.—There was no sign lacking which marked out the future judge.

Then suddenly Raicharan remembered that terrible accusation of the mother. "Ah," he said to himself with amazement, "the mother's heart was right. She knew I had stolen her child."

When once he had come to this conclusion, he was filled with remorse for his past neglect. He now gave himself over, body and soul, to the new baby and became its devoted attendant. He began to bring it up as if it were the son of a rich man. He bought a go-cart, a yellow satin waistcoat, and a gold-embroidered cap. He melted down the ornaments of his dead wife and made gold bangles and anklets. He refused to let the little child play with any one of the neighbourhood and became himself its sole companion day and night. As the baby grew up to boyhood, he was so petted and spoilt and clad in such finery that the village children would call him "Your Lordship," and jeer at him;

and older people regarded Raicharan as unaccountably crazy about the child.

At last the time came for the boy to go to school. Raicharan sold his small piece of land and went to Calcutta. There he got employment with great difficulty as a servant and sent Phailna to school. He spared no pains to give him the best education, the best clothes, the best food. Meanwhile, he himself lived on a mere handful of rice and would say in secret: "Ah, my little Master, my dear little Master, you loved me so much that you came back to my house! You shall never suffer from any neglect of mine."

Twelve years passed away in this manner. The boy was able to read and write well. He was bright and healthy and good-looking. He paid a great deal of attention to his personal appearance and was specially careful in parting his hair. He was inclined to extravagance and finery and spent money freely. He could never quite look on Raicharan as a father, because, though fatherly in affection, he had the manner of a servant. A further fault was this, that Raicharan kept secret from every one that he himself was the father of the child.

The students of the hostel, where Phailna was a boarder, were greatly amused by Raicharan's country manners, and I have to confess that behind his father's back Phailna joined in their fun. But, in the bottom of their hearts, all the students loved the innocent and tender-hearted old man, and Phailna was very fond of him also. But, as I have said before, he loved him with a kind of condescension.

Raicharan grew older and older, and his employer was continually finding fault with him for his incompetent work. He had been starving himself for the boy's sake, so he had grown physically weak and no longer up to his daily task. He would forget things and his mind became dull and stupid. But his employer expected a full servant's work out of him and would not brook excuses. The money that Raicharan had brought with him from the sale of his land was exhausted. The boy was continually grumbling about his clothes and asking for more money.

III

Raicharan made up his mind. He gave up the situation where he was working as a servant, and left some money with Phailna and said: "I have some business to do at home in my village, and shall be back soon."

He went off at once to Baraset where Anukul was magistrate. Anukul's wife was still broken down with grief. She had had no other child.

One day Anukul was resting after a long and weary day in court. His wife was buying, at an exorbitant price, a herb from a mendicant quack, which was said to ensure the birth of a child. A voice of greeting was heard in the courtyard. Anukul went out to see who was there. It was Raicharan. Anukul's heart was softened when he saw his old servant. He asked him many questions and offered to take him back into service.

Raicharan smiled faintly and said in reply: "I want to make obeisance to my mistress."

Anukul went with Raicharan into the house, where the mistress did not receive him as warmly as his old master. Raicharan took no notice of this, but folded his hands and said: "It was not the Padma that stole your baby. It was I."

Anukul exclaimed: "Great God! Eh! What! Where is he?"

Raicharan replied: "He is with me. I will bring him the day after to-morrow."

It was Sunday. There was no magistrate's court sitting. Both husband and wife were looking expectantly along the road, waiting from early morning for Raicharan's appearance. At ten o'clock he came leading Phailna by the hand.

Anukul's wife, without a question, took the boy into her lap and was wild with excitement, sometimes laughing, sometimes weeping, touching him, kissing his hair and his forehead, and gazing into his face with hungry, eager eyes. The boy was very good-looking and dressed like a gentleman's son. The heart of Anukul brimmed over with a sudden rush of affection.

Nevertheless the magistrate in him asked: "Have you any proofs?"

Raicharan said: "How could there be any proof of such a deed? God alone knows that I stole your boy, and no one else in the world."

When Anukul saw how eagerly his wife was clinging to the boy, he realised the futility of asking for proofs. It would be wiser to believe. And then,—where could an old man like Raicharan get such a boy from? And why should his faithful servant deceive him for nothing?

"But," he added severely, "Raicharan, you must not stay here."

"Where shall I go, Master?" said Raicharan, in a choking voice, folding his hands. "I am old. Who will take in an old man as a servant?"

The mistress said: "Let him stay. My child will be pleased. I forgive him."

But Anukul's magisterial conscience would not allow him. "No," he said, "he cannot be forgiven for what he has done."

Raicharan bowed to the ground and clasped Anukul's feet. "Master," he cried, "let me stay. It was not I who did it. It was God."

Anukul's conscience was more shocked than ever when Raicharan tried to put the blame on God's shoulders.

"No," he said, "I could not allow it. I cannot trust you any more. You have done an act of treachery."

Raicharan rose to his feet and said: "It was not I who did it."

"Who was it then?" asked Anukul.

Raicharan replied: "It was my fate."

But no educated man could take this for an excuse. Anukul remained obdurate.

When Phailna saw that he was the wealthy magistrate's son, and not Raicharan's, he was angry at first, thinking that he had been cheated all this time of his birthright. But seeing Raicharan in distress, he generously said to his father: "Father, forgive him. Even if you don't let him live with us, let him have a small monthly pension."

After hearing this, Raicharan did not utter another word. He looked for the last time on the face of his son. He made obeisance to his old master and mistress. Then he went out and was mingled with the numberless people of the world.

At the end of the month Anukul sent him some money to his village. But the money came back. There was no one there of the name of Raicharan.

MASTER MASHAI

I

Adhar Babu lives upon the interest of the capital left him by his father. Only the brokers, negotiating loans, come to his drawing room and smoke the silver-chased hookah, and the clerks from the attorney's office discuss the terms of some mortgage or the amount of the stamp fees. He is so careful with his money that even the most dogged efforts of the boys from the local football club fail to make any impression on his pocket.

At the time this story opens a new guest came into his household. After a long period of despair, his wife, Nanibala, bore him a son.

The child resembled his mother,—large eyes, well-formed nose, and fair complexion. Ratikanta, Adharlal's protégé, gave verdict,—"He is worthy of this noble house." They named him Venugopal.

Never before had Adharlal's wife expressed any opinion differing from her husband's on household expenses. There had been a hot discussion now and then about the propriety of some necessary item and up to this time she had merely acknowledged defeat with silent contempt. But now Adharlal could no longer maintain his supremacy. He had to give way little by little when things for his son were in question.

II

As Venugopal grew up, his father gradually became accustomed to spending money on him. He obtained an old teacher, who had a considerable repute for his learning and also for his success in dragging impassable boys through their examinations. But such a training does not lead to the cultivation of amiability. This man tried his best to win the boy's heart, but the little that was left in him of the natural milk of human kindness had turned sour, and the child repulsed his advances from the very beginning. The mother, in consequence, objected to him strongly, and complained that the very sight of him made her boy ill. So the teacher left.

Just then, Haralal made his appearance with a dirty dress and a torn pair of old canvas shoes. Haralal's mother, who was a widow, had kept him with great difficulty at a District school out of the scanty earnings which she made by cooking in strange houses and husking rice. He managed to pass the Matriculation and determined to go to College. As a result of his half-starved condition, his pinched face tapered to a point in an unnatural manner,—like Cape Comorin in the map of India; and the only broad portion of it was his forehead, which resembled the ranges of the Himalayas.

The servant asked Haralal what he wanted, and he answered timidly that he wished to see the master.

The servant answered sharply: "You can't see him." Haralal was hesitating, at a loss what to do next, when Venugopal, who had finished his game in the garden, suddenly came to the door. The servant shouted at Haralal: "Get away." Quite unaccountably Venugopal grew excited and cried: "No, he shan't get away." And he dragged the stranger to his father.

Adharlal had just risen from his mid-day sleep and was sitting quietly on the upper verandah in his cane chair, rocking his legs. Ratikanta was enjoying his hookah, seated in a chair next to him. He asked Haralal how far he had got in his reading. The young man bent his head and answered that he had passed the Matriculation. Ratikanta looked stern and expressed surprise that he should be so backward for his age. Haralal kept silence. It was Ratikanta's special pleasure to torture his patron's dependants, whether actual or potential.

Suddenly it struck Adharlal that he would be able to employ this youth as a tutor for his son on next to nothing. He agreed, there and then, to take him at a salary of five rupees a month with board and lodging free.

III

This time the post of tutor remained occupied longer than before. From the very beginning of their acquaintance Haralal and his pupil became great friends. Never before did Haralal have such an opportunity of loving any young human creature. His mother had been so poor and dependent, that he had never had the privilege of playing with the children where she was employed at work. He had not hitherto suspected the hidden stores of love which lay all the while accumulating in his own heart.

Venu, also, was glad to find a companion in Haralal. He was the only boy in the house. His two younger sisters were looked down upon, as unworthy of being his playmates. So his new tutor became his only companion, patiently bearing the undivided weight of the tyranny of his child friend.

IV

Venu was now eleven. Haralal had passed his Intermediate, winning a scholarship. He was working hard for his B.A. degree. After College lectures were over, he would take Venu out into the public park and tell him stories about the heroes from Greek History and Victor Hugo's romances. The child used to get quite impatient to run to Haralal, after school hours, in spite of his mother's attempts to keep him by her side.

This displeased Nanibala. She thought that it was a deep-laid plot of Haralal's to captivate her boy, in order to prolong his own appointment. One day she talked to him from behind the purdah: "It is your duty to teach my son only for an hour or two in the morning and evening. But why are you always with him? The child has nearly forgotten his own parents. You must understand that a man of your position is no fit companion for a boy belonging to this house."

Haralal's voice choked a little as he answered that for the future he would merely be Venu's teacher and would keep away from him at other times.

It was Haralal's usual practice to begin his College study early before dawn. The child would come to him directly after he had washed himself. There was a small pool in the garden and they used to feed the fish in it with puffed rice. Venu was also engaged in building a miniature garden-house, at the corner of the garden, with its liliputian gates and hedges and gravel paths. When the sun became too hot they would go back into the house, and Venu would have his morning lesson from Haralal.

On the day in question Venu had risen earlier than usual, because he wished to hear the end of the story which Haralal had begun the evening before. But he found his teacher absent. When asked about him, the door-servant said that he had gone out. At lesson time Venu remained unnaturally quiet. He never even asked Haralal why he had gone out, but went on mechanically with his lessons. When the child was with his mother taking his breakfast, she asked him what had happened to make him so gloomy, and why he was not eating his food. Venu gave no answer. After his meal his mother caressed him and questioned him repeatedly. Venu burst out crying and said,—"Master Mashai." His mother asked Venu,—"What about Master Mashai?" But Venu found it difficult to name the offence which his teacher had committed.

His mother said to Venu: "Has your Master Mashai been saying anything to you against me?"

Venu could not understand the question and went away.

V

There was a theft in Adhar Babu's house. The police were called in to investigate. Even Haralal's trunks were searched. Ratikanta said with meaning: "The man who steals anything, does not keep his thefts in his own box."

Adharlal called his son's tutor and said to him: "It will not be convenient for me to keep any of you in my own house. From to-day you will have to take up your quarters outside, only coming in to teach my son at the proper time."

Ratikanta said sagely, drawing at his hookah: "That is a good proposal,—good for both parties."

Haralal did not utter a word, but he sent a letter saying that it would be no longer possible for him to remain as tutor to Venu.

When Venu came back from school, he found his tutor's room empty. Even that broken steel trunk of his was absent. The rope was stretched across the corner, but there were no clothes or towel hanging on it. Only on the table, which formerly was strewn with books and papers, stood a bowl containing some gold-fish with a label on which was written the word "Venu" in Haralal's hand-writing. The boy ran up at once to his father and asked him what had happened. His father told him that Haralal had resigned his post. Venu went to his room and flung himself down and began to cry. Adharlal did not know what to do with him.

The next day, when Haralal was sitting on his wooden bedstead in the Hostel, debating with himself whether he should attend his college lectures, suddenly he saw Adhar Babu's servant coming into his room followed by Venu. Venu at once ran up to him and threw his arms round his neck asking him to come back to the house.

Haralal could not explain why it was absolutely impossible for him to go back, but the memory of those clinging arms and that pathetic request used to choke his breath with emotion long after.

VI

Haralal found out, after this, that his mind was in an unsettled state, and that he had but a small chance of winning the scholarship, even if he could pass the examination. At the same time, he knew that, without the scholarship, he could not continue his studies. So he tried to get employment in some office.

Fortunately for him, an English Manager of a big merchant firm took a fancy to him at first sight. After only a brief exchange of words the Manager asked him if he had any experience, and could he bring any testimonial. Haralal could only answer "No"; nevertheless a post was offered him of twenty rupees a month and fifteen rupees were allowed him in advance to help him to come properly dressed to the office.

The Manager made Haralal work extremely hard. He had to stay on after office hours and sometimes go to his master's house late in the evening. But, in this way, he learnt his work quicker than others, and his fellow clerks became jealous of him and tried to injure him, but without effect. He rented a small house in a narrow lane and brought his mother to live with him as soon as his salary was raised to forty rupees a month. Thus happiness came back to his mother after weary years of waiting.

Haralal's mother used to express a desire to see Venugopal, of whom she had heard so much. She wished to prepare some dishes with her own hand and to ask him to come just once to dine with her son. Haralal avoided the subject by saying that his house was not big enough to invite him for that purpose.

VII

The news reached Haralal that Venu's mother had died. He could not wait a moment, but went at once to Adharlal's house to see Venu. After that they began to see each other frequently.

But times had changed. Venu, stroking his budding moustache, had grown quite a young man of fashion. Friends, befitting his present condition, were numerous. That old dilapidated study chair and ink-stained desk had vanished, and the room now seemed to be bursting with pride at its new acquisitions,—its looking-glasses, oleographs, and other furniture. Venu had entered college, but showed no haste in crossing the boundary of the Intermediate examination.

Haralal remembered his mother's request to invite Venu to dinner. After great hesitation, he did so. Venugopal, with his handsome face, at once won the mother's heart. But as soon as ever the meal was over he became impatient to go, and looking at his gold watch he explained that he had pressing engagements elsewhere. Then he jumped into his carriage, which was waiting at the door, and drove away. Haralal with a sigh said to himself that he would never invite him again.

VIII

One day, on returning from office, Haralal noticed the presence of a man in the dark room on the ground floor of his house. Possibly he would have passed him by, had not the heavy scent of some foreign perfume attracted his attention. Haralal asked who was there, and the answer came:

"It is I, Master Mashai."

"What is the matter, Venu?" said Haralal. "When did you arrive?"

"I came hours ago," said Venu. "I did not know that you returned so late."

They went upstairs together and Haralal lighted the lamp and asked Venu whether all was well. Venu replied that his college classes were becoming a fearful bore, and his father did not realize how dreadfully hard it was for him to go on in the same class, year after year, with students much younger than himself. Haralal asked him what he wished to do. Venu then told him that he wanted to go to England and become a barrister. He gave an instance of a student, much less advanced than himself, who was getting ready to go. Haralal asked him if he had received his father's permission. Venu replied that his father would not hear a word of it until he had passed the Intermediate, and that was an impossibility in his present frame of mind. Haralal suggested that he himself should go and try to talk over his father.

"No," said Venu, "I can never allow that!"

Haralal asked Venu to stay for dinner and while they were waiting he gently placed his hand on Venu's shoulder and said:

"Venu, you should not quarrel with your father, or leave home."

Venu jumped up angrily and said that if he was not welcome, he could go elsewhere. Haralal caught him by the hand and implored him not to go away without taking his food. But Venu snatched away his hand and was just leaving the room when Haralal's mother brought the food in on a tray. On seeing Venu about to leave she pressed him to remain and he did so with bad grace.

While he was eating the sound of a carriage stopping at the door was heard. First a servant entered the room with creaking shoes and then Adhar Babu himself. Venu's face became pale. The mother left the room as soon as she saw strangers enter. Adhar Babu called out to Haralal in a voice thick with anger:

"Ratikanta gave me full warning, but I could not believe that you had such devilish cunning hidden in you. So, you think you're going to live upon Venu? This is sheer kidnapping, and I shall prosecute you in the Police Court."

Venu silently followed his father and went out of the house.

IX

The firm to which Haralal belonged began to buy up large quantities of rice and dhal from the country districts. To pay for this, Haralal had to take the cash every Saturday morning by the early train and disburse it. There were special centres where the brokers and middlemen would come with their receipts and accounts for settlement. Some discussion had taken place in the office about Haralal being entrusted with this work, without any security, but the Manager undertook all the responsibility and said that a security was not needed. This special work used to go on from the middle of December to the middle of April. Haralal would get back from it very late at night.

One day, after his return, he was told by his mother that Venu had called and that she had persuaded him to take his dinner at their house. This happened more than once. The mother said that it was because Venu missed his own mother, and the tears came into her eyes as she spoke about it.

One day Venu waited for Haralal to return and had a long talk with him.

"Master Mashai!" he said. "Father has become so cantankerous of late that I cannot live with him any longer. And, besides, I know that he is getting ready to marry again. Ratikanta is seeking a suitable match, and they are always conspiring about it. There used to be a time when my father would get anxious, if I were absent from home even for a few hours. Now, if I am away for more than a week, he takes no notice,—indeed he is greatly relieved. If this marriage takes place, I feel that I cannot live in the house any longer. You must show me a way out of this. I want to become independent."

Haralal felt deeply pained, but he did not know how to help his former pupil. Venu said that he was determined to go to England and become a barrister. Somehow or other he must get the passage money out of his father: he could borrow it on a note of hand and his father would have to pay when the creditors filed a suit. With this borrowed money he would get away, and when he was in England his father was certain to remit his expenses.

"But who is there," Haralal asked, "who would advance you the money?"

"You!" said Venu.

"I!" exclaimed Haralal in amazement.

"Yes," said Venu, "I've seen the servant bringing heaps of money here in bags."

"The servant and the money belong to someone else."

Haralal explained why the money came to his house at night, like birds to their nest, to be scattered next morning.

"But can't the Manager advance the sum?" Venu asked.

"He may do so," said Haralal, "if your father stands security."

The discussion ended at this point.

X

One Friday night a carriage and pair stopped before Haralal's lodging house. When Venu was announced Haralal was counting money in his bedroom, seated on the floor. Venu entered the room dressed in a strange manner. He had discarded his Bengali dress and was wearing a Parsee coat and trousers and had a cap on his head. Rings were prominent on almost all the fingers of both hands, and a thick gold chain was hanging round his neck: there was a gold-watch in his pocket, and diamond studs could be seen peeping from his shirt sleeves. Haralal at once asked him what was the matter and why he was wearing that dress.

"My father's marriage," said Venu, "comes off to-morrow. He tried hard to keep it from me, but I found it out. I asked him to allow me to go to our garden-house at Barrackpur for a few days, and he was only too glad to get rid of me so easily. I am going there, and I wish to God I had never to come back."

Haralal looked pointedly at the rings on his fingers. Venu explained that they had belonged to his mother. Haralal then asked him if he had already had his dinner. He answered, "Yes, haven't you had yours?"

"No," said Haralal, "I cannot leave this room until I have all the money safely locked up in this iron chest."

"Go and take your dinner," said Venu, "while I keep guard here: your mother will be waiting for you."

For a moment Haralal hesitated, and then he went out and had his dinner. In a short time he came back with his mother and the three of them sat among the bags of money talking together. When it was about midnight, Venu took out his watch and looked at it and jumped up saying that he would miss his train. Then he asked Haralal to keep all his rings and his watch and chain until he asked for them again. Haralal put them all together in a leather bag and laid it in the iron safe. Venu went out.

The canvas bags containing the currency notes had already been placed in the safe: only the loose coins remained to be counted over and put away with the rest.

XI

Haralal lay down on the floor of the same room, with the key under his pillow, and went to sleep. He dreamt that Venu's mother was loudly reproaching him from behind the curtain. Her words were indistinct, but rays of different colours from the jewels on her body kept piercing the curtain like needles and violently vibrating. Haralal struggled to call Venu, but his voice seemed to forsake him. At last, with a noise, the curtain fell down. Haralal started up from his sleep and found darkness piled up round about him. A sudden gust of wind had flung open the window and put out the light. Haralal's whole body was wet with perspiration. He relighted the lamp and saw, by the clock, that it was four in the morning. There was no time to sleep again; for he had to get ready to start.

After Haralal had washed his face and hands his mother called from her own room,—"Baba, why are you up so soon?"

It was the habit of Haralal to see his mother's face the first thing in the morning in order to bring a blessing upon the day. His mother said to him: "I was dreaming that you were going out to bring back a bride for yourself." Haralal went to his own bedroom and began to take out the bags containing the silver and the currency notes.

Suddenly his heart stopped beating. Three of the bags appeared to be empty. He knocked them against the iron safe, but this only proved his fear to be true. He opened them and shook them with all his might. Two letters from Venu dropped out from one of the bags. One was addressed to his father and one to Haralal.

Haralal tore open his own letter and began reading. The words seemed to run into one another. He trimmed the lamp, but felt as if he could not understand what he read. Yet the purport of the letter was clear. Venu had taken three thousand rupees, in currency notes, and had started for England. The steamer was to sail before day-break that very morning. The letter ended with the words: "I am explaining everything in a letter to my father. He will pay off the debt; and then, again, my mother's ornaments, which I have left in your care, will more than cover the amount I have taken."

Haralal locked up his room and hired a carriage and went with all haste to the jetty. But he did not know even the name of the steamer which Venu had taken. He ran the whole length of the wharves from Prinsep's Ghat to Metiaburuj. He found that two steamers had started on their voyage to England early that morning. It was impossible for him to know which of them carried

Venu, or how to reach him.

When Haralal got home, the sun was strong and the whole of Calcutta was awake. Everything before his eyes seemed blurred. He felt as if he were pushing against a fearful obstacle which was bodiless and without pity. His mother came on the verandah to ask him anxiously where he had gone. With a dry laugh he said to her,—"To bring home a bride for myself," and then he fainted away.

On opening his eyes after a while, Haralal asked his mother to leave him. Entering his room he shut the door from the inside while his mother remained seated on the floor of the verandah in the fierce glare of the sun. She kept calling to him fitfully, almost mechanically,—"Baba, Baba!"

The servant came from the Manager's office and knocked at the door, saying that they would miss the train if they did not start out at once. Haralal called from inside, "It will not be possible for me to start this morning."

"Then where are we to go, Sir?"

"I will tell you later on."

The servant went downstairs with a gesture of impatience.

Suddenly Haralal thought of the ornaments which Venu had left behind. Up till now he had completely forgotten about them, but with the thought came instant relief. He took the leather bag containing them, and also Venu's letter to his father, and left the house.

Before he reached Adharlal's house he could hear the bands playing for the wedding, yet on entering he could feel that there had been some disturbance. Haralal was told that there had been a theft the night before and one or two servants were suspected. Adhar Babu was sitting in the upper verandah flushed with anger and Ratikanta was smoking his hookah. Haralal said to Adhar Babu, "I have something private to tell you." Adharlal flared up, "I have no time now!" He was afraid that Haralal had come to borrow money or to ask his help. Ratikanta suggested that if there was any delicacy in making the request in his presence he would leave the place. Adharlal told him angrily to sit where he was. Then Haralal handed over the bag which Venu had left behind. Adharlal asked what was inside it and Haralal opened it and gave the contents into his hands.

Then Adhar Babu said with a sneer: "It's a paying business that you two have started—you and your former pupil! You were certain that the stolen property would be traced, and so you come along with it to me to claim a reward!"

Haralal presented the letter which Venu had written to his father. This only made Adharlal all the more furious.

"What's all this?" he shouted, "I'll call for the police! My son has not yet come of age,—and you have smuggled him out of the country! I'll bet my soul you've lent him a few hundred rupees, and then taken a note of hand for three thousand! But I am not going to be bound by this!"

"I never advanced him any money at all," said Haralal.

"Then how did he find it?" said Adharlal, "Do you mean to tell me he broke open your safe and stole it?"

Haralal stood silent.

Ratikanta sarcastically remarked: "I don't believe this fellow ever set hands on as much as three thousand rupees in his life."

When Haralal left the house he seemed to have lost the power of dreading anything, or even of being anxious. His mind seemed to refuse to work. Directly he entered the lane he saw a carriage waiting before his own lodging. For a moment he felt certain that it was Venu's. It was impossible to believe that his calamity could be so hopelessly final.

Haralal went up quickly, but found an English assistant from the firm sitting inside the carriage. The man came out when he saw Haralal and took him by the hand and asked him: "Why didn't you go out by train this morning?" The servant had told the Manager his suspicions and he had sent this man to find out.

Haralal answered: "Notes to the amount of three thousand rupees are missing."

The man asked how that could have happened.

Haralal remained silent.

The man said to Haralal: "Let us go upstairs together and see where you keep your money." They went up to the room and counted the money and made a thorough search of the house.

When the mother saw this she could not contain herself any longer. She came out before the stranger and said: "Baba, what has happened?" He answered in broken Hindustani that some money had been stolen.

"Stolen!" the mother cried, "Why! How could it be stolen? Who could do such a dastardly thing?" Haralal said to her: "Mother, don't say a word."

The man collected the remainder of the money and told Haralal to come with him to the Manager. The mother barred the way and said:

"Sir, where are you taking my son? I have brought him up, starving and straining to do honest work. My son would never touch money belonging to others."

The Englishman, not knowing Bengali, said, "Achcha! Achcha!" Haralal told his mother not to be anxious; he would explain it all to the Manager and soon be back again. The mother entreated him, with a distressed voice,

"Baba, you haven't taken a morsel of food all morning." Haralal stepped into the carriage and drove away, and the mother sank to the ground in the anguish of her heart.

The Manager said to Haralal: "Tell me the truth. What did happen?"

Haralal said to him, "I haven't taken any money."

"I fully believe it," said the Manager, "but surely you know who has taken it."

Haralal looked on the ground and remained silent.

"Somebody," said the Manager, "must have taken it away with your connivance."

"Nobody," replied Haralal, "could take it away with my knowledge without taking first my life."

"Look here, Haralal," said the Manager, "I trusted you completely. I took no security. I employed you in a post of great responsibility. Every one in the office was against me for doing so. The three thousand rupees is a small matter, but the shame of all this to me is a great matter. I will do one thing. I will give you the whole day to bring back this money. If you do so, I shall say nothing about it and I will keep you on in your post."

It was now eleven o'clock. Haralal with bent head went out of the office. The clerks began to discuss the affair with exultation.

"What can I do? What can I do?" Haralal repeated to himself, as he walked along like one dazed, the sun's heat pouring down upon him. At last his mind ceased to think at all about what could be done, but the mechanical walk went on without ceasing.

This city of Calcutta, which offered its shelter to thousands and thousands of men had become like a steel trap. He could see no way out. The whole body of people were conspiring to surround and hold him captive—this most insignificant of men, whom no one knew. Nobody had any special grudge against him, yet everybody was his enemy. The crowd passed by, brushing against him: the clerks of the offices were eating their lunch on the road side from their plates made of leaves: a tired wayfarer on the Maidan, under the shade of a tree, was lying with one hand beneath his head and one leg upraised over the other: The up-country women, crowded into hackney carriages, were wending their way to the temple: a chuprassie came up with a letter and asked him the address on the envelope,—so the afternoon went by.

Then came the time when the offices were all about to close. Carriages started off in all directions, carrying people back to their homes. The clerks, packed tightly on the seats of the trams, looked at the theatre advertisements as they returned to their lodgings. From to-day, Haralal had neither his work in the office, nor release from work in the evening. He had no need to hurry to catch the tram to take him to his home. All the busy occupations of the city—the buildings—the horses and carriages—the incessant traffic—seemed, now at one time, to swell into dreadful reality, and at another time, to subside into the shadowy unreal.

Haralal had taken neither food, nor rest, nor shelter all that day.

The street lamps were lighted from one road to another and it seemed to him that a watchful darkness, like some demon, was keeping its eyes wide open to guard every movement of its victim. Haralal did not even have the energy to enquire how late it was. The veins on his forehead throbbed, and he felt as if his head would burst. Through the paroxysms of pain, which alternated with the apathy of dejection, only one thought came again and again to his mind; among the innumerable multitudes in that vast city, only one name found its way through his dry throat,—"Mother!"

He said to himself, "At the deep of night, when no one is awake to capture me—me, who am the least of all men,—I will silently creep to my mother's arms and fall asleep, and may I never wake again!"

Haralal's one trouble was lest some police officer should molest him in the presence of his mother, and this kept him back from going home. When it became impossible for him at last to bear the weight of his own body, he hailed a carriage. The driver asked him where he wanted to go. He said: "Nowhere, I want to drive across the Maidan to get the fresh air." The man at first did not believe him and was about to drive on, when Haralal put a rupee into his hand as an advance payment. Thereupon the driver crossed, and then re-crossed, the Maidan from one side to the other, traversing the different roads.

Haralal laid his throbbing head on the side of the open window of the carriage and closed his eyes. Slowly all the pain abated. His body became cool. A deep and intense peace filled his heart and a supreme deliverance seemed to embrace him on every side. It was not true,—the day's despair which threatened him with its grip of utter helplessness. It was not true, it was false. He knew now that it was only an empty fear of the mind. Deliverance was in the infinite sky and there was no end to peace. No king or emperor in the world had the power to keep captive this nonentity, this Haralal. In the sky, surrounding his emancipated heart on every side, he felt the presence of his mother, that one poor woman. She seemed to grow and grow till she filled the infinity of darkness. All the roads and buildings and shops of Calcutta gradually became enveloped by her. In her presence vanished all the aching pains and thoughts and consciousness of Haralal. It burst,—that bubble filled with the hot vapour of pain. And now there was neither darkness nor light, but only one tense fulness.

The Cathedral clock struck one. The driver called out impatiently: "Babu, my horse can't go on any longer. Where do you want to go?"

There came no answer.

The driver came down and shook Haralal and asked him again where he wanted to go.

There came no answer.

And the answer was never received from Haralal, where he wanted to go.

SUBHA

When the girl was given the name of Subhashini, who could have guessed that she would prove dumb? Her two elder sisters were Sukeshini and Suhasini, and for the sake of uniformity her father named his youngest girl Subhashini. She was called Subha for short.

Her two elder sisters had been married with the usual cost and difficulty, and now the youngest daughter lay like a silent weight upon the heart of her parents. All the world seemed to think that, because she did not speak, therefore she did not feel; it discussed her future and its own anxiety freely in her presence. She had understood from her earliest childhood that God had sent her like a curse to her father's house, so she withdrew herself from ordinary people and tried to live apart. If only they would all forget her she felt she could endure it. But who can forget pain? Night and day her parents' minds were aching on her account. Especially her mother looked upon her as a deformity in herself. To a mother a daughter is a more closely intimate part of herself than a son can be; and a fault in her is a source of personal shame. Banikantha, Subha's father, loved her rather better than his other daughters; her mother regarded her with aversion as a stain upon her own body.

If Subha lacked speech, she did not lack a pair of large dark eyes, shaded with long lashes; and her lips trembled like a leaf in response to any thought that rose in her mind.

When we express our thought in words, the medium is not found easily. There must be a process of translation, which is often inexact, and then we fall into error. But black eyes need no translating; the mind itself throws a shadow upon them. In them thought opens or shuts, shines forth or goes out in darkness, hangs steadfast like the setting moon or like the swift and restless lightning illumines all quarters of the sky. They who from birth have had no other speech than the trembling of their lips learn a language of the eyes, endless in expression, deep as the sea, clear as the heavens, wherein play dawn and sunset, light and shadow. The dumb have a lonely grandeur like Nature's own. Wherefore the other children almost dreaded Subha and never played with her. She was silent and companionless as noontide.

The hamlet where she lived was Chandipur. Its river, small for a river of Bengal, kept to its narrow bounds like a daughter of the middle class. This busy streak of water never overflowed its banks, but went about its duties as though it were a member of every family in the villages beside it. On either side were houses and banks shaded with trees. So stepping from her queenly throne, the river-goddess became a garden deity of each home, and forgetful of herself performed her task of endless benediction with swift and cheerful foot.

Banikantha's house looked out upon the stream. Every hut and stack in the place could be seen by the passing boatmen. I know not if amid these signs of worldly wealth any one noticed the little girl who, when her work was done, stole away to the waterside and sat there. But here Nature fulfilled her want of speech and spoke for her. The murmur of the brook, the voice of the village folk, the songs of the boatmen, the crying of the birds and rustle of trees mingled and were one with the trembling of her heart. They became one vast wave of sound which beat upon her restless soul. This murmur and movement of Nature were the dumb girl's language; that speech of the dark eyes, which the long lashes shaded, was the language of the world about her. From the trees, where the cicalas chirped, to the quiet stars there was nothing but signs and gestures, weeping and sighing. And in the deep mid-noon, when the boatmen and fisher-folk had gone to their dinner, when the villagers slept and birds were still, when the ferry-boats were idle, when the great busy world paused in its toil and became suddenly a lonely, awful giant, then beneath the vast impressive heavens there were only dumb Nature and a dumb girl, sitting very silent,—one under the spreading sunlight, the other where a small tree cast its shadow.

But Subha was not altogether without friends. In the stall were two cows, Sarbbashi and Panguli. They had never heard their names from her lips, but they knew her footfall. Though she had no words, she murmured lovingly and they understood her gentle murmuring better than all speech. When she fondled them or scolded or coaxed them, they understood her better than men could do. Subha would come to the shed and throw her arms round Sarbbashi's neck; she would rub her cheek against her friend's, and Panguli would turn her great kind eyes and lick her face. The girl paid them three regular visits every day and others that were irregular. Whenever she heard any words that hurt her, she would come to these dumb friends out of due time. It was as though they guessed her anguish of spirit from her quiet look of sadness. Coming close to her, they would rub their horns softly against her arms, and in dumb, puzzled fashion try to comfort her. Besides these two, there were goats and a kitten; but Subha had not the same equality of friendship with them, though they showed the same attachment. Every time it got a chance, night or day, the kitten would jump into her lap, and settle down to slumber, and show its appreciation of an aid to sleep as Subha drew her soft fingers over its neck and back.

Subha had a comrade also among the higher animals, and it is hard to say what were the girl's relations with him; for he could speak, and his gift of speech left them without any common language. He was the youngest boy of the Gosains, Pratap by name, an idle fellow. After long effort, his parents had abandoned the hope that he would ever make his living. Now losels have this advantage, that, though their own folk disapprove of them, they are generally popular with every one else. Having no work to chain them, they become public property. Just as every town needs an open space where all may breathe, so a village needs two or three gentlemen of leisure, who can give time to all; then, if we are lazy and want a companion, one is to hand.

Pratap's chief ambition was to catch fish. He managed to waste a lot of time this way, and might be seen almost any afternoon so employed. It was thus most often that he met Subha. Whatever he was about, he liked a companion; and, when one is catching fish, a silent companion is best of all. Pratap respected Subha for her taciturnity, and, as every one called her Subha, he showed his affection by calling her Su. Subha used to sit beneath a tamarind, and Pratap, a little distance off, would cast his line. Pratap took with him a small allowance of betel, and Subha prepared it for him. And I think that, sitting and gazing a long while, she desired ardently to bring some great help to Pratap, to be of real aid, to prove by any means that she was not a useless burden to the world. But there was nothing to do. Then she turned to the Creator in prayer for some rare power, that by an astonishing miracle she might startle Pratap into exclaiming: "My! I never dreamt our Su could have done this!"

Only think, if Subha had been a water nymph, she might have risen slowly from the river, bringing the gem of a snake's crown to the landing-place. Then Pratap, leaving his paltry fishing, might dive into the lower world, and see there, on a golden bed in a palace of silver, whom else but dumb little Su, Banikantha's child? Yes, our Su, the only daughter of the king of that shining city of jewels! But that might not be, it was impossible. Not that anything is really impossible, but Su had been born, not into the royal house of Patalpur, but into Banikantha's family, and she knew no means of astonishing the Gosains' boy.

Gradually she grew up. Gradually she began to find herself. A new inexpressible consciousness like a tide from the central places of the sea, when the moon is full, swept through her. She saw herself, questioned herself, but no answer came that she could understand.

Once upon a time, late on a night of full moon, she slowly opened her door and peeped out timidly. Nature, herself at full moon, like lonely Subha, was looking down on the sleeping earth. Her strong young life beat within her; joy and sadness filled her being to its brim; she reached the limits even of her own illimitable loneliness, nay, passed beyond them. Her heart was heavy, and she could not speak. At the skirts of this silent troubled Mother there stood a silent troubled girl.

The thought of her marriage filled her parents with an anxious care. People blamed them, and even talked of making them outcasts. Banikantha was well off; they had fish-curry twice daily; and consequently he did not lack enemies. Then the women interfered, and Bani went away for a few days. Presently he returned and said: "We must go to Calcutta."

They got ready to go to this strange country. Subha's heart was heavy with tears, like a mist-wrapt dawn. With a vague fear that had been gathering for days, she dogged her father and mother like a dumb animal. With her large eyes wide open, she scanned their faces as though she wished to learn something. But not a word did they vouchsafe. One afternoon in the midst of all this, as Pratap was fishing, he laughed: "So then, Su, they have caught your bridegroom, and you are going to be married! Mind you don't forget me altogether!" Then he turned his mind again to his fish. As a stricken doe looks in the hunter's face, asking in silent agony: "What have I done to you?" so Subha looked at Pratap. That day she sat no longer beneath her tree. Banikantha, having finished his nap, was smoking in his bedroom when Subha dropped down at his feet and burst out weeping as she gazed towards him. Banikantha tried to comfort her, and his cheek grew wet with tears.

It was settled that on the morrow they should go to Calcutta. Subha went to the cow-shed to bid farewell to her childhood's comrades. She fed them with her hand; she clasped their necks; she looked into their faces, and tears fell fast from the eyes which spoke for her. That night was the tenth of the moon. Subha left her room, and flung herself down on her grassy couch beside her dear river. It was as if she threw her arms about Earth, her strong silent mother, and tried to say: "Do not let me leave you, mother. Put your arms about me, as I have put mine about you, and hold me fast."

One day in a house in Calcutta, Subha's mother dressed her up with great care. She imprisoned her hair, knotting it up in laces, she hung her about with ornaments, and did her best to kill her natural beauty. Subha's eyes filled with tears. Her mother, fearing they would grow swollen with weeping, scolded her harshly, but the tears disregarded the scolding. The bridegroom came with a friend to inspect the bride. Her parents were dizzy with anxiety and fear when they saw the god arrive to select the beast for his sacrifice. Behind the stage, the mother called her instructions aloud, and increased her daughter's weeping twofold, before she sent her into the examiner's presence. The great man, after scanning her a long time, observed: "Not so bad."

He took special note of her tears, and thought she must have a tender heart. He put it to her credit in the account, arguing that the heart, which to-day was distressed at leaving her parents, would presently prove a useful possession. Like the oyster's pearls, the child's tears only increased her value, and he made no other comment.

The almanac was consulted, and the marriage took place on an auspicious day. Having delivered over their dumb girl into another's hands, Subha's parents returned home. Thank God! Their caste in this and their safety in the next world were assured! The bridegroom's work lay in the west, and shortly after the marriage he took his wife thither.

In less than ten days every one knew that the bride was dumb! At least, if any one did not, it was not her fault, for she deceived no one. Her eyes told them everything, though no one understood her. She looked on every hand, she found no speech, she missed the faces, familiar from birth, of those who had understood a dumb girl's language. In her silent heart there sounded an endless, voiceless weeping, which only the Searcher of Hearts could hear.

THE CASTAWAY

Towards evening the storm was at its height. From the terrific downpour of rain, the crash of thunder, and the repeated flashes of lightning, you might think that a battle of the gods and demons was raging in the skies. Black clouds waved like the Flags of Doom. The Ganges was lashed into a fury, and the trees of the gardens on either bank swayed from side to side with sighs and groans.

In a closed room of one of the riverside houses at Chandernagore, a husband and his wife were seated on a bed spread on the floor, intently discussing. An earthen lamp burned beside them.

The husband, Sharat, was saying: "I wish you would stay on a few days more; you would then be able to return home quite strong again."

The wife, Kiran, was saying: "I have quite recovered already. It will not, cannot possibly, do me any harm to go home now."

Every married person will at once understand that the conversation was not quite so brief as I have reported it. The matter was not difficult, but the arguments for and against did not advance it towards a solution. Like a rudderless boat, the discussion kept turning round and round the same point; and at last threatened to be overwhelmed in a flood of tears.

Sharat said: "The doctor thinks you should stop here a few days longer."

Kiran replied: "Your doctor knows everything!"

"Well," said Sharat, "you know that just now all sorts of illnesses are abroad. You would do well to stop here a month or two more."

"And at this moment I suppose every one in this place is perfectly well!"

What had happened was this: Kiran was a universal favourite with her family and neighbours, so that, when she fell seriously ill, they were all anxious. The village wiseacres thought it shameless for her husband to make so much fuss about a mere wife and even to suggest a change of air, and asked if Sharat supposed that no woman had ever been ill before, or whether he had found out that the folk of the place to which he meant to take her were immortal. Did he imagine that the writ of Fate did not run there? But Sharat and his mother turned a deaf ear to them, thinking that the little life of their darling was of greater importance than the united wisdom of a village. People are wont to reason thus when danger threatens their loved ones. So Sharat went to Chandernagore, and Kiran recovered, though she was still very weak. There was a pinched look on her face which filled the beholder with pity, and made his heart tremble, as he thought how narrowly she had escaped death.

Kiran was fond of society and amusement; the loneliness of her riverside villa did not suit her at all. There was nothing to do, there were no interesting neighbours, and she hated to be busy all day with medicine and dieting. There was no fun in measuring doses and making fomentations. Such was the subject discussed in their closed room on this stormy evening.

So long as Kiran deigned to argue, there was a chance of a fair fight. When she ceased to reply, and with a toss of her head disconsolately looked the other way, the poor man was disarmed. He was on the point of surrendering unconditionally when a servant shouted a message through the shut door.

Sharat got up and on opening the door learnt that a boat had been upset in the storm, and that one of the occupants, a young Brahmin boy, had succeeded in swimming ashore at their garden.

Kiran was at once her own sweet self and set to work to get out some dry clothes for the boy. She then warmed a cup of milk and invited him to her room.

The boy had long curly hair, big expressive eyes, and no sign yet of hair on the face. Kiran, after getting him to drink some milk asked him all about himself.

He told her that his name was Nilkanta, and that he belonged to a theatrical troupe. They were coming to play in a neighbouring villa when the boat had suddenly foundered in the storm. He had no idea what had become of his companions. He was a good swimmer and had just managed to reach the shore.

The boy stayed with them. His narrow escape from a terrible death made Kiran take a warm interest in him. Sharat thought the boy's appearance at this moment rather a good thing, as his wife would now have something to amuse her, and might be persuaded to stay on for some time longer. Her mother-in-law, too, was pleased at the prospect of profiting their Brahmin guest by her kindness. And Nilkanta himself was delighted at his double escape from his master and from the other world, as well as at finding a home in this wealthy family.

But in a short while Sharat and his mother changed their opinion, and longed for his departure. The boy found a secret pleasure in smoking Sharat's hookahs; he would calmly go off in pouring rain with Sharat's best silk umbrella for a stroll through the village, and make friends with all whom he met. Moreover, he had got hold of a mongrel village dog which he petted so recklessly that it came indoors with muddy paws, and left tokens of its visit on Sharat's spotless bed. Then he gathered about him a devoted band of boys of all sorts and sizes, and the result was that not a solitary mango in the neighbourhood had a chance of ripening that season.

There is no doubt that Kiran had a hand in spoiling the boy. Sharat often warned her about it, but she would not listen to him. She made a dandy of him with Sharat's cast-off clothes, and gave him new ones also. And because she felt drawn towards him, and had a curiosity to know more about him, she was constantly calling him to her own room. After her bath and midday meal Kiran would be seated on the bedstead with her betel-leaf box by her side; and while her maid combed and dried her hair, Nilkanta would stand in front and recite pieces out of his repertory with appropriate gesture and song, his elf-locks waving wildly. Thus the long afternoon hours passed merrily away. Kiran would often try to persuade Sharat to sit with her as one of the audience, but Sharat, who had taken a cordial dislike to the boy, refused; nor could Nilkanta do his part half so well when Sharat was there. His mother would sometimes be lured by the hope of hearing sacred names in the recitation; but love of her mid-day sleep speedily overcame devotion, and she lay lapped in dreams.

The boy often got his ears boxed and pulled by Sharat, but as this was nothing to what he had been used to as a member of the troupe, he did not mind it in the least. In his short experience of the world he had come to the conclusion that, as the earth consisted of land and water, so human life was made up of eatings and beatings, and that the beatings largely predominated.

It was hard to tell Nilkanta's age. If it was about fourteen or fifteen, then his face was too old for his years; if seventeen or eighteen, then it was too young. He was either a man too early or a boy too late. The fact was that, joining the theatrical band when very young, he had played the parts of Radhika, Damayanti, and Sita, and a thoughtful Providence so arranged things that he grew to the exact stature that his manager required, and then growth ceased.

Since every one saw how small Nilkanta was, and he himself felt small, he did not receive due respect for his years. Causes, natural and artificial, combined to make him sometimes seem immature for seventeen years, and at other times a mere lad of fourteen but far too knowing even for seventeen. And as no sign of hair appeared on his face, the confusion became greater. Either because he smoked or because he used language beyond his years, his lips puckered into lines that showed him to be old and hard; but innocence and youth shone in his large eyes. I fancy that his heart remained young, but the hot glare of publicity had been a forcing-house that ripened untimely his outward aspect.

In the quiet shelter of Sharat's house and garden at Chandernagore, Nature had leisure to work her way unimpeded. Nilkanta had lingered in a kind of unnatural youth, but now he silently and swiftly overpassed that stage. His seventeen or eighteen years came to adequate revelation. No one observed the change, and its first sign was this, that when Kiran treated him like a boy, he felt ashamed. When the gay Kiran one day proposed that he should play the part of lady's companion, the idea of woman's dress hurt him, though he could not say why. So now, when she called for him to act over again his old characters, he disappeared.

It never occurred to Nilkanta that he was even now not much more than a lad-of-all-work in a strolling company. He even made up his mind to pick up a little education from Sharat's factor. But, because he was the pet of his master's wife, the factor could not endure the sight of him. Also, his restless training made it impossible for him to keep his mind long engaged; sooner or later, the alphabet did a misty dance before his eyes. He would sit long enough with an open book on his lap, leaning against a champak bush beside the Ganges. The waves sighed below, boats floated past, birds flitted and twittered restlessly above. What thoughts passed through his mind as he looked down on that book he alone knew, if indeed he did know. He never advanced from one word to another, but the glorious thought, that he was actually reading a book, filled his soul with exultation. Whenever a boat went by, he lifted his book, and pretended to be reading hard, shouting at the top of his voice. But his energy dropped as soon as the audience was gone.

Formerly he sang his songs automatically, but now their tunes stirred in his mind. Their words were of little import and full of trifling alliteration. Even the feeble meaning they had was beyond his comprehension; yet when he sang

Twice-born bird, ah! wherefore stirred
To wrong our royal lady?
Goose, ah, say why wilt thou slay
Her in forest shady?

then he felt as if transported to another world and to fear other folk. This familiar earth and his own poor life became music, and he was transformed. That tale of the goose and the king's daughter flung upon the mirror of his mind a picture of surpassing beauty. It is impossible to say what he imagined himself to be, but the destitute little slave of the theatrical troupe faded from his memory.

When with evening the child of want lies down, dirty and hungry, in his squalid home, and hears of prince and princess and fabled gold, then in the dark hovel with its dim flickering candle, his mind springs free from its bonds of poverty and misery and walks in fresh beauty and glowing raiment, strong beyond all fear of hindrance, through that fairy realm where all is possible.

Even so, this drudge of wandering players fashioned himself and his world anew, as he moved in spirit amid his songs. The lapping water, rustling leaves, and calling birds; the goddess who had given shelter to him, the helpless, the God-forsaken; her gracious, lovely face, her exquisite arms with their shining bangles, her rosy feet as soft as flower-petals; all these by some magic became one with the music of his song. When the singing ended, the mirage faded, and the Nilkanta of the stage appeared again, with his wild elf-locks. Fresh from the complaints of his neighbour, the owner of the despoiled mango-orchard, Sharat would come and box his ears and cuff him. The boy Nilkanta, the misleader of adoring youths, went forth once more, to make ever new mischief by land and water and in the branches that are above the earth.

Shortly after the advent of Nilkanta, Sharat's younger brother, Satish, came to spend his college vacation with them. Kiran was hugely pleased at finding a fresh occupation. She and Satish were of the same age, and the time passed pleasantly in games and quarrels and reconciliations and laughter and even tears. Suddenly she would clasp him over the eyes from behind with vermilion-stained hands, or she would write "monkey" on his back, or else she would bolt the door on him from the outside amidst peals of laughter. Satish in his turn did not take things lying down; he would steal her keys and rings; he would put pepper among her betel, he would tie her to the bed when she was not looking.

Meanwhile, heaven only knows what possessed poor Nilkanta. He was suddenly filled with a bitterness which he must avenge on somebody or something. He thrashed his devoted boy-followers for no fault, and sent them away crying. He would kick his pet mongrel till it made the skies resound with its whinings. When he went out for a walk, he would litter his path with twigs and leaves beaten from the roadside shrubs with his cane.

Kiran liked to see people enjoying good fare. Nilkanta had an immense capacity for eating, and never refused a good thing however often it was offered. So Kiran liked to send for him to have his meals in her presence, and ply him with delicacies, happy in the bliss of seeing this Brahmin boy eat to satiety. After Satish's arrival she had much less spare time on her hands, and was seldom present when Nilkanta's meals were served. Before, her absence made no difference to the boy's appetite, and he would not rise till he had drained his cup of milk and rinsed it thoroughly with water.

But now, if Kiran was not present to ask him to try this and that, he was miserable, and nothing tasted right. He would get up, without eating much, and say to the serving-maid in a choking voice: "I am not hungry." He thought in imagination that the news of his repeated refusal, "I am not hungry," would reach Kiran; he pictured her concern, and hoped that she would send for him, and press him to eat. But nothing of the sort happened. Kiran never knew and never sent for him; and the maid finished whatever he left. He would then put out the lamp in his room, and throw himself on his bed in the darkness, burying his head in the pillow in a paroxysm of sobs. What was his grievance? Against whom? And from whom did he expect redress? At last, when no one else came, Mother Sleep soothed with her soft caresses the wounded heart of the motherless lad.

Nilkanta came to the unshakable conviction that Satish was poisoning Kiran's mind against him. If Kiran was absent-minded, and had not her usual smile, he would jump to the conclusion that some trick of Satish had made her angry with him. He took to praying to the gods, with all the fervour of his hate, to make him at the next rebirth Satish, and Satish him. He had an idea that a Brahmin's wrath could never be in vain; and the more he tried to consume Satish with the fire of his curses, the more did his own heart burn within him. And upstairs he would hear Satish laughing and joking with his sister-in-law.

Nilkanta never dared openly to show his enmity to Satish. But he would contrive a hundred petty ways of causing him annoyance. When Satish went for a swim in the river, and left his soap on the steps of the bathing-place, on coming back for it he would find that it had disappeared. Once he found his favourite striped tunic floating past him on the water, and thought it had been blown away by the wind.

One day Kiran, desiring to entertain Satish, sent for Nilkanta to recite as usual, but he stood there in gloomy silence. Quite surprised, Kiran asked him what was the matter. But he remained silent. And when again pressed by her to repeat some particular favourite piece of hers, he answered: "I don't remember," and walked away.

At last the time came for their return home. Everybody was busy packing up. Satish was going with them. But to Nilkanta nobody said a word. The question whether he was to go or not seemed to have occurred to nobody.

The subject, as a matter of fact, had been raised by Kiran, who had proposed to take him along with them. But her husband and his mother and brother had all objected so strenuously that she let the matter drop. A couple of days before they were to start, she sent for the boy, and with kind words advised him to go back to his own home.

So many days had he felt neglected that this touch of kindness was too much for him; he burst into tears. Kiran's eyes were also brimming over. She was filled with remorse at the thought that she had created a tie of affection, which could not be permanent.

But Satish was much annoyed at the blubbering of this overgrown boy. "Why does the fool stand there howling instead of speaking?" said he. When Kiran scolded him for an unfeeling creature, he replied: "My dear sister, you do not understand. You are too good and trustful. This fellow turns up from the Lord knows where, and is treated like a king. Naturally the tiger has no wish to become a mouse again. And he has evidently discovered that there is nothing like a tear or two to soften your heart."

Nilkanta hurriedly left the spot. He felt he would like to be a knife to cut Satish to pieces; a needle to pierce him through and through; a fire to burn him to ashes. But Satish was not even scared. It was only his own heart that bled and bled.

Satish had brought with him from Calcutta a grand inkstand. The inkpot was set in a mother-of-pearl boat drawn by a German-silver goose supporting a penholder. It was a great favourite of his, and he cleaned it carefully every day with an old silk handkerchief. Kiran would laugh, and tapping the silver bird's beak would say

Twice-born bird, ah! wherefore stirred
To wrong our royal lady?

and the usual war of words would break out between her and her brother-in-law.

The day before they were to start, the inkstand was missing and could nowhere be found. Kiran smiled, and said: "Brother-in-law, your goose has flown off to look for your Damayanti."

But Satish was in a great rage. He was certain that Nilkanta had stolen it—for several people said they had seen him prowling about the room the night before. He had the accused brought before him. Kiran also was there. "You have stolen my inkstand, you thief!" he blurted out. "Bring it back at once." Nilkanta had always taken punishment from Sharat, deserved or undeserved, with perfect equanimity. But, when he was called a thief in Kiran's presence, his eyes blazed with a fierce anger, his breast swelled, and his throat choked. If Satish had said another word, he would have flown at him like a wild cat and used his nails like claws.

Kiran was greatly distressed at the scene, and taking the boy into another room said in her sweet, kind way: "Nilu, if you really have taken that inkstand give it to me quietly, and I shall see that no one says another word to you about it." Big tears coursed down the boy's cheeks, till at last he hid his face in his hands, and wept bitterly. Kiran came back from the room and said: "I am sure Nilkanta has not taken the inkstand." Sharat and Satish were equally positive that no other than Nilkanta could have done it.

But Kiran said determinedly: "Never."

Sharat wanted to cross-examine the boy, but his wife refused to allow it.

Then Satish suggested that his room and box should be searched. And Kiran said: "If you dare do such a thing I will never forgive you. You shall not spy on the poor innocent boy." And as she spoke, her wonderful eyes filled with tears. That settled the matter and effectually prevented any further molestation of Nilkanta.

Kiran's heart overflowed with pity at this attempted outrage on a homeless lad. She got two new suits of clothes and a pair of shoes, and with these and a banknote in her hand she quietly went into Nilkanta's room in the evening. She intended to put these parting presents into his box as a surprise. The box itself had been her gift.

From her bunch of keys she selected one that fitted and noiselessly opened the box. It was so jumbled up with odds and ends that the new clothes would not go in. So she thought she had better take everything out and pack the box for him. At first knives, tops, kite-flying reels, bamboo twigs, polished shells for peeling green mangoes, bottoms of broken tumblers and such like things dear to a boy's heart were discovered. Then there came a layer of linen, clean and otherwise. And from under the linen there emerged the missing inkstand, goose and all.

Kiran, with flushed face, sat down helplessly with the inkstand in her hand, puzzled and wondering.

In the meantime, Nilkanta had come into the room from behind without Kiran knowing it. He had seen the whole thing and thought that Kiran had come like a thief to catch him in his thieving,—and that his deed was out. How could he ever hope to convince her that he was not a thief, and that only revenge had prompted him to take the inkstand, which he meant to throw into the river at the first chance? In a weak moment he had put it in the box instead. "He was not a thief," his heart cried out, "not a thief!" Then what was he? What could he say? That he had stolen, and yet he was not a thief? He could never explain to Kiran how grievously wrong she was. And then, how could he bear the thought that she had tried to spy on him?

At last Kiran with a deep sigh replaced the inkstand in the box, and, as if she were the thief herself, covered it up with the linen and the trinkets as they were before; and at the top she placed the presents, together with the banknote which she had brought for him.

The next day the boy was nowhere to be found. The villagers had not seen him; the police could discover no trace of him. Said Sharat: "Now, as a matter of curiosity, let us have a look at his box." But Kiran was obstinate in her refusal to allow that to be done.

She had the box brought up to her own room; and taking out the inkstand alone, she threw it into the river.

The whole family went home. In a day the garden became desolate. And only that starving mongrel of Nilkanta's remained prowling along the river-bank, whining and whining as if its heart would break.

THE SON OF RASHMANI

I

Kalipada's mother was Rashmani, but she had to do the duty of the father as well, because when both of the parents are "mother" then it is bad for the child. Bhavani, her husband, was wholly incapable of keeping his children under discipline. To know why he was bent on spoiling his son, you must hear something of the former history of the family.

Bhavani was born in the famous house of Saniari. His father, Abhaya Charan, had a son, Shyama Charan, by his first wife. When he married again after her death he had himself passed the marriageable age, and his new father-in-law took advantage of the weakness of his position to have a special portion of his estate settled on his daughter. In this way he was satisfied that proper provision had been made, if his daughter should become a widow early in life. She would be independent of the charity of Shyama Charan.

The first part of his anticipation came true. For very soon after the birth of a son, whom she called Bhavani, Abhaya Charan died. It gave the father-in-law great peace and consolation, as he looked forward to his own death, to know that his daughter was properly looked after.

Shyama Charan was quite grown up. In fact his own eldest boy was a year older than Bhavani. He brought up the latter with his own son. In doing this he never took a farthing from the property allotted to his step-mother, and every year he got a receipt from her after submitting detailed accounts. His honesty in this affair surprised the neighbourhood. In fact they thought that such honesty was another name for foolishness. They did not like the idea of a division being made in the undivided ancestral property. If Shyama Charan in some underhand manner had been able to annul the dowry, his neighbours would have admired his sagacity; and there were good advisers ready to hand who could have rendered him material aid in the attainment of such an object.

But Shyama Charan, in spite of the risk of crippling his patrimony, strictly set aside the dowry which came to the share of his step-mother; and the widow, Vraja Sundari, being naturally affectionate and trustful, had every confidence in Shyama Charan whom she trusted as her own son. More than once she had chided him for being so particular about her portion of the property. She would tell him that, as she was not going to take her property with her when she died, and as it would in any case revert to the family, it was not necessary to be so very strict about rendering accounts. But he never listened to her.

Shyama Charan was a severe disciplinarian by habit and his children were perfectly aware of the fact. But Bhavani had every possible freedom, and this gave rise to the impression that he was more partial to his step-brother than to his own sons. But Bhavani's education was sadly neglected and he completely relied on Shyama Charan for the management of his share of the property. He merely had to sign documents occasionally without ever spending a thought on their contents. On the other hand, Tarapada, the eldest son of Shyama Charan, was quite an expert in the management of the estate, having to act as an assistant to his father.

After the death of Shyama Charan, Tarapada said to Bhavani, "Uncle, we must not live together as we have done for so long, because some trifling misunderstanding may come at any moment and cause utter disruption."

Bhavani never imagined, even in his dream, that a day might come when he would have to manage his own affairs. The world in which he had been born and bred ever appeared to him complete and entire in itself. It was an incomprehensible calamity to him that there could be a dividing line somewhere and that this world of his could be split into two. When he found that Tarapada was immovable and indifferent to the grief and dishonour that such a step would bring to the family, he began to rack his brain to find out how the property could be divided with the least possible strain.

Tarapada showed surprise at his uncle's anxiety and said that there was no need to trouble about this, because the division had already been made in the life-time of his grandfather. Bhavani said in amazement, "But I know nothing of this!" Tarapada said in answer, "Then you must be the only one in the whole neighbourhood who does not. For, lest there should be ruinous litigation after he had gone, my grandfather had already given a portion of the property to your mother." Bhavani thought this not unlikely and asked, "What about the house?" Tarapada said, "If you wish, you can keep this house to yourself and we shall be contented with the other house in the district town."

As Bhavani had never been to this town-house, he had neither knowledge of it, nor affection for it. He was astounded at the magnanimity of Tarapada for so easily relinquishing his right to the house in the village where they had been brought up. But when Bhavani told everything to his mother, she struck her forehead with her hand and said: "This is preposterous! What I got from my husband was my own dowry and its income is very small. I do not see why you should be deprived of your share in your father's property."

Bhavani said, "Tarapada is quite positive that his grandfather never gave us any thing except this land."

Vraja Sundari was astonished and informed her son that her husband had made two copies of his will, one of which was still lying in her own box. The box was opened and it was found that there was only the deed of gift for the property belonging to the mother and nothing else. The copy of the will had been taken out.

The help of advisers was sought. The man who came to their rescue was Bagala, the son of their family guru. It was the profession of the father to look after the spiritual needs of the village; the material side was left to the son. The two of them had divided between themselves the other world and this. Whatever might be the result for others, they themselves had nothing to suffer from this division. Bagala said that, even if the will was missing, the shares in the ancestral property must be equal, as between the brothers.

Just at this time, a copy of a will made its appearance supporting the claims of the other side. In this document there was no mention of Bhavani and the whole property was given to the grandsons at the time when no son was born to Bhavani. With Bagala as his captain Bhavani set out on his voyage across the perilous sea of litigation. When his vessel at last reached harbour his funds were nearly exhausted and the ancestral property was in the hands of the other party. The land which was given to his mother had dwindled to such an extent, that it could barely give them shelter, or keep up the family dignity. Then Tarapada went away to the district town and they never met again.

II

Shyama Charan's treachery pierced the heart of the widow like an assassin's knife. To the end of her life, almost every day she would heave a sigh and say that God would never suffer such an injustice to be done. She was quite firm in her faith when she said to Bhavani, "I do not know your law or your law courts, but I am certain that my husband's true will and testament will someday be recovered. You will find it again."

Because Bhavani was helpless in worldly matters such assurances as these gave him great consolation. He settled down in his inactivity, certain in his own mind that his pious mother's prophecy could never remain unfulfilled. After his mother's death his faith became all the stronger, since the memory of her piety acquired greater radiance through death's mystery. He felt quite unconcerned about the stress of their poverty which became more and more formidable as the years went by. The necessities of life and the maintenance of family traditions,—these seemed to him like play acting on a temporary stage, not real things. When his former expensive clothing was outworn and he had to buy cheap materials in the shop, this amused him almost like a joke. He smiled and said to himself,—"These people do not know that this is only a passing phase of my fortune. Their surprise will be all the greater, when some day I shall celebrate the Puja Festival with unwonted magnificence."

This certainty of future prodigality was so clear to his mind's eye that present penury escaped his attention. His servant, Noto, was the principal companion with whom he had discussions about these things. They used to have animated conversations, in which sometimes his opinion differed from his master's, as to the propriety of bringing down a theatrical troupe from Calcutta for these future occasions. Noto used to get reprimands from Bhavani for his natural miserliness in these items of future expenditure.

While Bhavani's one anxiety was about the absence of an heir, who could inherit his vast possible wealth, a son was born to him. The horoscope plainly indicated that the lost property would come back to this boy.

From the time of the birth of his son, Bhavani's attitude was changed. It became cruelly difficult for him now to bear his poverty with his old amused equanimity, because he felt that he had a duty towards this new representative of the illustrious house of Saniari, who had such a glorious future before him. That the traditional extravagance could not be maintained on the occasion of the birth of his child gave him the keenest sorrow. He felt as if he were cheating his own son. So he compensated his boy with an inordinate amount of spoiling.

Bhavani's wife, Rashmani, had a different temperament from her husband. She never felt any anxiety about the family traditions of the Chowdhuris of Saniari. Bhavani was quite aware of the fact and indulgently smiled to himself, as though nothing better could be expected from a woman who came from a Vaishnava family of very humble lineage. Rashmani frankly acknowledged that she could not share the family sentiments: what concerned her most was the welfare of her own child.

There was hardly an acquaintance in the neighbourhood with whom Bhavani did not discuss the question of the lost will; but he never spoke a word about it to his wife. Once or twice he had tried, but her perfect unconcern had made him drop the subject. She neither paid attention to the past greatness of the family, nor to its future glories,—she kept her mind busy with the actual necessities of the present, and those necessities were not small in number or quality.

When the Goddess of Fortune deserts a house, she usually leaves some of her burdens behind, and this ancient family was still encumbered with its host of dependents, though its own shelter was nearly crumbling to dust. These parasites take it to be an insult if they are asked to do any service. They get head-aches at the least touch of the kitchen smoke. They are visited with sudden rheumatism the moment they are asked to run errands. Therefore all the responsibilities of maintaining the family were laid upon Rashmani herself. Women lose their delicacy of refinement, when they are compelled night and day to haggle with their destiny over things which are pitifully small, and for this they are blamed by those for whom they toil.

Besides her household affairs Rashmani had to keep all the accounts of the little landed property which remained and also to make arrangements for collecting rents. Never before was the estate managed with such strictness. Bhavani had been quite incapable of collecting his dues: Rashmani never made any remission of the least fraction of rent. The tenants, and even her own agents, reviled her behind her back for the meanness of the family from which she came. Even her husband occasionally used to enter his protest against the harsh economy which went against the grain of the world-famed house of Saniari.

Rashmani quite ungrudgingly took the blame of all this upon herself and openly confessed the poverty of her parents. Tying the end of her sari tightly round her waist she went on with her household duties in her own vigorous fashion and made herself thoroughly disagreeable both to the inmates of the house and to her neighbours. But nobody ever had the courage to interfere. Only one thing she carefully avoided. She never asked her husband to help her in any work and she was nervously afraid of his taking up any responsibilities. Indeed she was always furiously engaged in keeping her husband idle; and because he had received the best possible training in this direction she was wholly successful in her mission.

Rashmani had attained middle age before her son came. Up to this time all the pent-up tenderness of the mother in her and all the love of the wife had their centre of devotion in this simple-hearted good-for-nothing husband. Bhavani was a child grown up by mistake beyond its natural age. This was the reason why, after the death of her husband's mother, she had to assume the position of mother and mistress in one.

In order to protect her husband from invasions of Bagala, the son of the guru, and other calamities, Rashmani adopted such a stern demeanour, that the companions of her husband used to be terribly afraid of her. She never had the opportunity, which a woman usually has, of keeping her fierceness hidden and of softening the keen edge of her words,—maintaining a dignified reserve towards men such as is proper for a woman.

Bhavani meekly accepted his wife's authority with regard to himself, but it became extremely hard for him to obey her when it related to Kalipada, his son. The reason was, that Rashmani never regarded Bhavani's son from the point of view of Bhavani himself. In her heart she pitied her husband and said, "Poor man, it was no fault of his, but his misfortune, to be born into a rich family." That is why she never could expect her husband to be deprived of any comfort to which he had been accustomed. Whatever might be the condition of the household finance, she tried hard to keep him in his habitual ease and luxury. Under her régime all expense was strictly limited except in the case of Bhavani. She would never allow him to notice if some inevitable gap occurred in the preparation of his meals or his apparel. She would blame some imaginary dog for spoiling dishes that were never made and would blame herself for her carelessness. She would attack Noto for letting some fictitious article of dress be stolen or lost. This had the usual effect of rousing Bhavani's sympathy on behalf of his favourite servant and he would take up his defence. Indeed it had often happened that Bhavani had confessed with bare-faced shamelessness that he had used the dress which had never been bought, and for whose loss Noto was blamed; but what happened afterwards, he had not the power to invent and was obliged to rely upon the fertile imagination of his wife who was also the accuser!

Thus Rashmani treated her husband, but she never put her son in the same category. For he was her own child and why should he be allowed to give himself airs? Kalipada had to be content for his breakfast with a few handfuls of puffed rice and some treacle. During the cold weather he had to wrap his body as well as his head with a thick rough cotton chaddar. She would call his teacher before her and warn him never to spare her boy, if he was the least neglectful with his lessons. This treatment of his own son was the hardest blow that Bhavani Charan suffered since the days of his destitution. But as he had always acknowledged defeat at the hands of the powerful, he had not the spirit to stand up against his wife in her method of dealing with the boy.

The dress which Rashmani provided for her son, during the Puja festivities, was made of such poor material that in former days the very servants of the house would have rebelled if it had been offered to them. But Rashmani more than once tried her best to explain to her husband that Kalipada, being the most recent addition to the Chowdhuri family, had never known their former splendour and so was quite glad to get what was given to him. But this pathetic innocence of the boy about his own destiny hurt Bhavani more than anything else, and he could not forgive himself for deceiving the child. When Kalipada would dance for joy and rush to him to show him some present from his mother, which was ridiculously trivial, Bhavani's heart would suffer torture.

Bagala, the guru's son, was now in an affluent condition owing to his agency in the law suit which had brought about the ruin of Bhavani. With the money which he had in hand he used to buy cheap tinsel wares from Calcutta before the Puja holidays. Invisible ink,—absurd combinations of stick, fishing-rod and umbrella,—letter-paper with pictures in the corner,—silk fabrics bought at auctions, and other things of this kind, attractive to the simple villagers,—these were his stock in trade. All the forward young men of the village vied with one another in rising above their rusticity by purchasing these sweepings of the Calcutta market which, they were told, were absolutely necessary for the city gentry.

Once Bagala had bought a wonderful toy,—a doll in the form of a foreign woman,—which, when wound up, would rise from her chair and begin to fan herself with sudden alacrity. Kalipada was fascinated by it. He had a very good reason to avoid asking his mother about the toy; so he went straight to his father and begged him to purchase it for him. Bhavani answered "yes" at once, but when he heard the price his face fell. Rashmani kept all the money and he went to her as a timid beggar. He began with all sorts of irrelevant remarks and then took a desperate plunge into the subject with startling incoherence.

Rashmani briefly remarked: "Are you mad?" Bhavani Charan sat silent revolving in his mind what to say next.

"Look here," he exclaimed, "I don't think I need milk pudding daily with my dinner."

"Who told you?" said Rashmani sharply.

"The doctor says it's very bad for biliousness."

"The doctor's a fool!"

"But I'm sure that rice agrees with me better than your luchis. They are too indigestible."

"I've never seen the least sign of indigestion in you. You have been accustomed to them all your life!"

Bhavani Charan was ready enough to make sacrifices, but there his passage was barred. Butter might rise in price, but the number of his luchis never diminished. Milk was quite enough for him at his midday meal, but curds also had to be supplied because that was the family tradition. Rashmani could not have borne seeing him sit down to his meal, if curds were not supplied. Therefore all his attempts to make a breach in his daily provisions, through which the fanning foreign woman might enter, were an utter failure.

Then Bhavani paid a visit to Bagala for no reason whatever, and after a great deal of round about talk asked concerning the foreign doll. Of course his straightened circumstances had long been known to Bagala, yet it was a perfect misery to Bhavani to have to hesitate to buy this doll for his son owing to want of ready money. Swallowing his pride, he brought out from under his arm an expensive old Kashmir shawl, and said in a husky voice: "My circumstances are bad just at present and I haven't got much cash. So I have determined to mortgage this shawl and buy that doll for Kalipada."

If the object offered had been less expensive than this Kashmir shawl, Bagala would at once have closed the bargain. But knowing that it would not be possible for him to take possession of this shawl in face of the village opinion, and still more in face of Rashmani's watchfulness, he refused to accept it; and Bhavani had to go back home disappointed with the Kashmir shawl hidden under his arm.

Kalipada asked every day for that foreign fanning toy, and Bhavani smiled every day and said,—"Wait, a bit, my boy, till the seventh day of the moon comes round." But every new day it became more and more difficult to keep up that smile.

On the fourth day of the moon Bhavani made a sudden inroad upon his wife and said:

“I’ve noticed that there’s something wrong with Kalipada,—something the matter with his health.”

“Nonsense,” said Rashmani, “he’s in the best of health.”

“Haven’t you noticed him sitting silent for hours together?”

“I should be very greatly relieved if he could sit still for as many minutes.”

When all his arrows had missed their mark, and no impression had been made, Bhavani Charan heaved a deep sigh and passing his fingers through his hair went away and sat down on the verandah and began to smoke with fearful assiduity.

On the fifth day, at his morning meal, Bhavani passed by the curds and the milk pudding without touching them. In the evening he simply took one single piece of sandesh. The luchis were left unheeded. He complained of want of appetite. This time a considerable breach was made in the fortifications.

On the sixth day, Rashmani took Kalipada into the room and sweetly calling him by his pet name said, “Betu, you are old enough to know that it is the halfway house to stealing to desire that which you can’t have.”

Kalipada whimpered and said, “What do I know about it? Father promised to give me that doll.”

Rashmani sat down to explain to him how much lay behind his father’s promise,—how much pain, how much affection, how much loss and privation. Rashmani had never in her life before talked thus to Kalipada, because it was her habit to give short and sharp commands. It filled the boy with amazement when he found his mother coaxing him and explaining things at such a length, and mere child though he was, he could fathom something of the deep suffering of his mother’s heart. Yet at the same time it will be easily understood, that it was hard for this boy to turn his mind away altogether from that captivating foreign fanning woman. He pulled a long face and began to scratch the ground.

This made Rashmani’s heart at once hard, and she said in her severe tone: “Yes, you may weep and cry, or become angry, but you shall never get that which is not for you to have.” And she hastened away without another word.

Kalipada went out. Bhavani Charan was still smoking his hookah. Noticing Kalipada from a distance he got up and walked in the opposite direction as if he had some urgent business. Kalipada ran to him and said,—"But that doll?" Bhavani could not raise a smile that day. He put his arm round Kalipada's neck and said:

"Baba, wait a little. I have some pressing business to get through. Let me finish it first, and then we will talk about it." Saying this, he went out of his house.

Kalipada saw him brush a tear from his eyes. He stood at the door and watched his father, and it was quite evident, even to this boy, that he was going nowhere in particular, and that he was dragging the weight of a despair which could not be relieved.

Kalipada at once went back to his mother and said:

"Mother, I don't want that foreign doll."

That morning Bhavani Charan returned late. When he sat down to his meal, after his bath, it was quite evident, by the look on his face, that the curds and the milk pudding would fare no better with him than on the day before, and that the best part of the fish would go to the cat.

Just at this critical juncture Rashmani brought in a card-board box, bound round with twine, and set it before her husband. Her intention had been to reveal the mystery of this packet to her husband when he went to take his nap after his meal. But in order to remove the undeserved neglect of the curds and the milk and the fish, she had to disclose its contents before the time. So the foreign doll came out of the box and without more ado began to fan itself vigorously.

After this, the cat had to go away disappointed. Bhavani remarked to his wife that the cooking was the best he had ever tasted. The fish soup was incomparable: the curds had set themselves with an exactness that was rarely attained, and the milk pudding was superb.

On the seventh day of the moon, Kalipada got the toy for which he had been pining. During the whole of that day he allowed the foreigner to go on fanning herself and thereby made his boy companions jealous. In any other case this performance would have seemed to him monotonously tiresome, but knowing that on the following day he would have to give the toy back, his constancy to it on that single occasion remained unabated. At the rental of two rupees per diem Rashmani had hired it from Bagala.

On the eighth day of the moon, Kalipada heaved a deep sigh and returned the toy, along with the box and twine, to Bagala with his own hands. From that day forward Kalipada began to share the confidences of his mother, and it became so absurdly easy for Bhavani to give expensive presents every year, that it surprised even himself.

When, with the help of his mother, Kalipada came to know that nothing in this world could be gained without paying for it with the inevitable price of suffering, he rapidly grew up in his mind and became a valued assistant to his mother in her daily tasks. It come to be a natural rule of life with him that no one should add to the burden of the world, but that each should try to lighten it.

When Kalipada won a scholarship at the Vernacular examination, Bhavani proposed that he should give up his studies and take in hand the supervision of the estate. Kalipada went to his mother and said,—"I shall never be a man, if I do not complete my education."

The mother said,—"You are right, Baba, you must go to Calcutta."

Kalipada explained to her that it would not be necessary to spend a single pice on him; his scholarship would be sufficient, and he would try to get some work to supplement it.

But it was necessary to convince Bhavani of the wisdom of the course. Rashmani did not wish to employ the argument that there was very little of the estate remaining to require supervision; for she knew how it would hurt him. She said that Kalipada must become a man whom everyone could respect. But all the members of the Chowdhuri family had attained their respectability without ever going a step outside the limits of Saniari. The outer world was as unknown to them as the world beyond the grave. Bhavani, therefore, could not conceive how anybody could think of a boy like Kalipada going to Calcutta. But the cleverest man in the village, Bagala, fortunately agreed with Rashmani.

"It is perfectly clear," he said, "that, one day, Kalipada will become a lawyer; and then he will set matters right concerning the property of which the family has been deprived."

This was a great consolation to Bhavani Charan and he brought out the file of records about the theft of the will and tried to explain the whole thing to Kalipada by dint of daily discussion. But his son was lacking in proper enthusiasm and merely echoed his father's sentiment about this solemn wrong.

The day before Kalipada's departure for Calcutta Rashmani hung round his neck an amulet containing some mantras to protect him from evils. She gave him at the same time a fifty-rupee currency note, advising him to keep it for any special emergency. This note, which was the symbol of his mother's numberless daily acts of self-denial, was the truest amulet of all for Kalipada. He determined to keep it by him and never to spend it, whatever might happen.

III

From this time onward the old interminable discussions about the theft of the will became less frequent on the part of Bhavani. His one topic of conversation was the marvellous adventure of Kalipada in search of his education. Kalipada was actually engaged in his studies in the city of Calcutta! Kalipada knew Calcutta as well as the palm of his hand! Kalipada had been the first to hear the great news that another bridge was going to be built over the Ganges near Hughli! The day on which the father received his son's letter, he would go to every house in the village to read it to his neighbours and he would hardly find time even to take his spectacles from his nose. On arriving at a fresh house he would remove them from their case with the utmost deliberation; then he would wipe them carefully with the end of his dhoti; then, word by word, he would slowly read the letter through to one neighbour after another, with something like the following comment:—

"Brother, just listen! What is the world coming to? Even the dogs and the jackals are to cross the holy Ganges without washing the dust from their feet! Who could imagine such a sacrilege?"

No doubt it was very deplorable; but all the same it gave Bhavani Charan a peculiar pleasure to communicate at first hand such important news from his own son's letter, and this more than compensated for the spiritual disaster which must surely overtake the numberless creatures of this present age. To everyone he met he solemnly nodded his head and prophesied that the days were soon coming when Mother Ganges would disappear altogether; all the while cherishing the hope that the news of such a momentous event would come to him by letter from his own son in the proper time.

Kalipada, with very great difficulty, scraped together just enough money to pay his expenses till he passed his Matriculation and again won a scholarship. Bhavani at once made up his mind to invite all the village to a feast, for he imagined that his son's good ship of fortune had now reached its haven and there would be no more occasion for economy. But he received no encouragement from Rashmani.

Kalipada was fortunate enough to secure a place of study in a students' lodging house near his college. The proprietor allowed him to occupy a small room on the ground floor which was absolutely useless for other lodgers. In exchange for this and his board, he had to coach the son of the owner of the house. The one great advantage was that there would be no chance of any fellow lodger ever sharing his quarters. So, although ventilation was lacking, his studies were uninterrupted.

Those of the students who paid their rent and lived in the upper story had no concern with Kalipada; but soon it became painfully evident that those who are up above have the power to hurl missiles at those below with all the more deadly force because of their distance. The leader of those above was Sailen.

Sailen was the scion of a rich family. It was unnecessary for him to live in a students' mess, but he successfully convinced his guardians that this would be best for his studies. The real reason was that Sailen was naturally fond of company, and the students' lodging house was an ideal place where he could have all the pleasure of companionship without any of its responsibilities. It was the firm conviction of Sailen that he was a good fellow and a man of feeling. The advantage of harbouring such a conviction was that it needed no proof in practice. Vanity is not like a horse or an elephant requiring expensive fodder.

Nevertheless, as Sailen had plenty of money he did not allow his vanity merely to graze at large; he took special pride in keeping it stall-fed. It must be said to his credit that he had a genuine desire to help people in their need, but the desire in him was of such a character, that if a man in difficulty refused to come to him for help, he would turn round on him and do his best to add to his trouble. His mess mates had their tickets for the theatre bought for them by Sailen, and it cost them nothing to have occasional feasts. They could borrow money from him without meaning to pay it back. When a newly married youth was in doubt about the choice of some gift for his wife, he could fully rely on Sailen's good taste in the matter. On these occasions the love-lorn youth would take Sailen to the shop and pretend to select the cheapest and least suitable presents: then Sailen, with a contemptuous laugh would intervene and select the right thing. At the mention of the price the young husband would pull a long face, but Sailen would always be ready to abide by his own superior choice and to pay the cost.

In this manner Sailen became the acknowledged patron of the students upstairs. It made him intolerant of the insolence of any one who refused to accept his help. Indeed, to help others in this way had become his hobby.

Kalipada, in his tattered jersey, used to sit on a dirty mat in his damp room below and recite his lessons, swinging himself from side to side to the rhythm of the sentence. It was a sheer necessity for him to get that scholarship next year.

Kalipada's mother had made him promise, before he left home for Calcutta that he would avoid the company of rich young men. Therefore he bore the burden of his indigence alone, strictly keeping himself from those who had been more favoured by fortune. But to Sailen, it seemed a sheer impertinence that a student as poor as Kalipada should yet have the pride to keep away from his patronage. Besides this, in his food and dress and everything, Kalipada's poverty was so blatantly exposed, it hurt Sailen's sense of decency. Every time he looked down into Kalipada's room, he was offended by the sight of the cheap clothing, the dingy mosquito net and the tattered bedding. Whenever he passed on his way to his own room in the upper story the sight of these things was unavoidable. To crown it all there was that absurd amulet which Kalipada always had hanging round his neck, and those daily rites of devotion which were so ridiculously out of fashion!

One day Sailen and his followers condescended to invite Kalipada to a feast, thinking that his gratitude would know no bounds. But Kalipada sent an answer saying that his habits were different and it would not be wholesome for him to accept the invitation. Sailen was unaccustomed to such a refusal, and it roused up in him all the ferocity of his insulted benevolence. For some days after this, the noise on the upper story became so loudly insistent that it was impossible for Kalipada to go on with his studies. He was compelled to spend the greater part of his days studying in the Park, and to get up very early and sit down to his work long before it was light.

Owing to his half-starved condition, his mental overwork, and badly-ventilated room, Kalipada began to suffer from continual attacks of headache. There were times when he was obliged to lie down on his bed for three or four days together. But he made no mention of his illness in his letters to his father. Bhavani himself was certain that, just as vegetation grew rank in his village surroundings, so comforts of all kinds sprang up of themselves from the soil of Calcutta. Kalipada never for a moment disabused his mind of that misconception. He did not fail to write to his father, even when suffering from one of these paroxysms of pain. The deliberate rowdiness of the students in the upper story added at such times to his distress.

Kalipada tried to make himself as scarce and small as possible, in order to avoid notice; but this did not bring him relief. One day, he found that a cheap shoe of his own had been taken away and replaced by an expensive foreign one. It was impossible for him to go to college with such an incongruous pair. He made no complaint, however, but bought some old second-hand shoes from the cobbler. One day, a student from the upper story came into his room and asked him:

"Have you, by any mistake, brought away my silver cigarette case with you?"

Kalipada got annoyed and answered:

"I have never been inside your room in my life."

The student stooped down. "Hullo!" he said, "here it is!" And the valuable cigarette case was picked up from the corner of the room.

Kalipada determined to leave this lodging house as soon as ever he had passed his Intermediate Examination, provided only he could get a scholarship to enable him to do so.

Every year the students of the house used to have their annual Saraswati Puja. Though the greater part of the expenses fell to the share of Sailen, every one else contributed according to his means. The year before, they had contemptuously left out Kalipada from the list of contributors; but this year, merely to tease him, they came with their subscription book. Kalipada instantly paid five rupees to the fund, though he had no intention of participating in the feast. His penury had long brought on him the contempt of his fellow lodgers, but this unexpected gift of five rupees became to them insufferable. The Saraswati Puja was performed with great éclat and the five rupees could easily have been spared. It had been hard indeed for Kalipada to part with it. While he took the food given him in his landlord's house he had no control over the time at which it was served. Besides this, since the servants brought him the food, he did not like to criticise the dishes. He preferred to provide himself with some extra things; and after the forced extravagance of his five-rupee subscription he had to forgo all this and suffered in consequence. His paroxysms of headache became more frequent, and though he passed his examination, he failed to obtain the scholarship that he desired.

The loss of the scholarship drove Kalipada to do extra work as a private tutor and to stick to the same unhealthy room in the lodging house. The students overhead had hoped that they would be relieved of his presence. But punctually to the day the room was unlocked on the lower floor. Kalipada entered, clad in the same old dirty check Parsee coat. A coolie from Sealdah Station took down from his head a steel trunk and other miscellaneous packages and laid them on the floor of the room; and a long wrangle ensued as to the proper amount of pice that were due.

In the depths of those packages there were mango chutnies and other condiments which his mother had specially prepared. Kalipada was aware that, in his absence, the upper-story students, in search of a jest, did not scruple to come into his room by stealth.

He was especially anxious to keep these home gifts from their cruel scrutiny. As tokens of home affection they were supremely precious to him; but to the town students, they denoted merely the boorishness of poverty-stricken villagers. The vessels were crude and earthen, fastened up by an earthen lid fixed on with paste of flour. They were neither glass nor porcelain, and therefore sure to be regarded with insolent disdain by rich town-bred people.

Formerly Kalipada used to keep these stores hidden under his bed, covering them up with old newspapers. But this time he took the precaution of always locking up his door, even if he went out for a few minutes. This still further roused the spleen of Sailen and his party. It seemed to them preposterous that the room which was poor enough to draw tears from the eyes of the most hardened burglar should be as carefully guarded as if it were a second Bank of Bengal.

"Does he actually believe," they said among themselves, "that the temptation will be irresistible for us to steal that Parsee coat?"

Sailen had never visited this dark and mildewed room from which the plaster was dropping. The glimpses that he had taken, while going upstairs,—especially when, in the evening, Kalipada, the upper part of his body bare, would sit poring over his books with a smoky lamp beside him,—were enough to give him a sense of suffocation. Sailen asked his boon companions to explore the room below and find out the treasure which Kalipada had hidden. Everybody felt intensely amused at the proposal.

The lock on Kalipada's door was a cheap one, which had the magnanimity to lend itself to any key. One evening when Kalipada had gone out to his private tuition, two or three of the students with an exuberant sense of humour took a lantern and unlocked the room and entered. It did not need a moment to discover the pots of chutney under the bed, but these hardly seemed valuable enough to demand such watchful care on the part of Kalipada. A further search disclosed a key on a ring under the pillow. They opened the steel trunk with the key and found a few soiled clothes, books and writing material. They were about to shut the box in disgust when they saw, at the very bottom, a packet covered by a dirty handkerchief. On uncovering three or four wrappers they found a currency note of fifty rupees. This made them burst out into peals of laughter. They felt certain that Kalipada was harbouring suspicion against the whole world in his mind because of this fifty rupees!

The meanness of this suspicious precaution deepened the intensity of their contempt for Kalipada. Just then, they heard a foot-step outside. They hastily shut the box, locked the door, and ran upstairs with the note in their possession.

Sailen was vastly amused. Though fifty rupees was a mere trifle, he could never have believed that Kalipada had so much money in his trunk. They all decided to watch the result of this loss upon that queer creature downstairs.

When Kalipada came home that night after his tuition was over, he was too tired to notice any disorder in his room. One of his worst attacks of nervous headache was coming on and he went straight to bed.

The next day, when he brought out his trunk from under the bed and took out his clothes, he found it open. He was naturally careful, but it was not unlikely, he thought, that he had forgotten to lock it on the day before. But when he lifted the lid he found all the contents topsy-turvy, and his heart gave a great thud when he discovered that the note, given to him by his mother, was missing. He searched the box over and over again in the vain hope of finding it, and when his loss was made certain, he flung himself upon his bed and lay like one dead.

Just then, he heard footsteps following one another on the stairs, and every now and then an outburst of laughter from the upper room. It struck him, all of a sudden, that this was not a theft: Sailen and his party must have taken the note to amuse themselves and make laughter out of it. It would have given him less pain if a thief had stolen it. It seemed to him that these young men had laid their impious hands upon his mother herself.

This was the first time that Kalipada had ascended those stairs. He ran to the upper floor,—the old jersey on his shoulders,—his face flushed with anger and the pain of his illness. As it was Sunday, Sailen and his company were seated in the verandah, laughing and talking. Without any warning, Kalipada burst upon them and shouted:

"Give me back my note!"

If he had begged it of them, they would have relented; but the sight of his anger made them furious. They started up from their chairs and exclaimed:
"What do you mean, sir? What do you mean? What note?"

Kalipada shouted: "The note you have taken from my box!"

"How dare you?" they shouted back. "Do you take us to be thieves?"

If Kalipada had held any weapon in his hand at that moment he certainly would have killed some one among them. But when he was about to spring, they fell on him, and four or five of them dragged him down to his room and thrust him inside.

Sailen said to his companions: "Here, take this hundred-rupee note, and throw it to that dog!"

They all loudly exclaimed: "No! Let him climb down first and give us a written apology. Then we shall consider it!"

Sailen's party all went to bed at the proper time and slept the sleep of the innocent. In the morning they had almost forgotten Kalipada. But some of them, while passing his room, heard the sound of talking and they thought that possibly he was busy consulting some lawyer. The door was shut from the inside. They tried to overhear, but what they heard had nothing legal about it. It was quite incoherent.

They informed Sailen. He came down and stood with his ear close to the door. The only thing that could be distinctly heard was the word 'Father.' This frightened Sailen. He thought that possibly Kalipada had gone mad on account of the grief of losing that fifty-rupee note. Sailen shouted "Kalipada Babu!" two or three times, but got no answer. Only that muttering sound continued. Sailen called,—"Kalipada Babu,—please open the door. Your note has been found." But still the door was not opened and that muttering sound went on.

Sailen had never anticipated such a result as this. He did not express a word of repentance to his followers, but he felt the sting of it all the same. Some advised him to break open the door: others thought that the police should be called in,—for Kalipada might be in a dangerous state of lunacy. Sailen at once sent for a doctor who lived close at hand. When they burst open the door they found the bedding hanging from the bed and Kalipada lying on the floor unconscious. He was tossing about and throwing up his arms and muttering, with his eyes red and open and his face all flushed. The doctor examined him and asked if there were any relative near at hand; for the case was serious.

Sailen answered that he knew nothing, but would make inquiries. The doctor then advised the removal of the patient at once to an upstairs room and proper nursing arrangements day and night. Sailen took him up to his own room and dismissed his followers. He got some ice and put it on Kalipada's head and began to fan him with his own hand.

Kalipada, fearing that mocking references would be made, had concealed the names and address of his parents from these people with special care. So Sailen had no alternative but to open his box. He found two bundles of letters tied up with ribbon. One of them contained his mother's letters, the other contained his father's. His mother's letters were fewer in number than his father's. Sailen closed the door and began to read the letters. He was startled when he saw the address,—Saniari, the house of the Chowdhuries,—and then the name of the father, Bhavani. He folded up the letters and sat still, gazing at Kalipada's face. Some of his friends had casually mentioned, that there was a resemblance between Kalipada and himself. But he was offended at the remark and did not believe it. To-day he discovered the truth. He knew that his own grandfather, Shyama Charan, had a step-brother named Bhavani; but the later history to the family had remained a secret to him. He did not even know that Bhavani had a son named Kalipada; and he never suspected that Bhavani had come to such an abject state of poverty as this. He now felt not only relieved, but proud of his own relative, Kalipada, that he had refused to enter himself on the list of protégés.

IV

Knowing that his party had insulted Kalipada almost every day, Sailen felt reluctant to keep him in the lodging house with them. So he rented another suitable house and kept him there. Bhavani came down in haste to Calcutta the moment he received a letter from Sailen informing him of his son's illness. Rashmani parted with all her savings giving instructions to her husband to spare no expense upon her son. It was not considered proper for the daughters of the great Chowdhuri family to leave their home and go to Calcutta unless absolutely obliged, and therefore she had to remain behind offering prayers to all the tutelary gods. When Bhavani Charan arrived he found Kalipada still unconscious and delirious. It nearly broke Bhavani's heart when he heard himself called 'Master Mashai.' Kalipada often called him in his delirium and he tried to make himself recognized by his son, but in vain.

The doctor came again and said the fever was getting less. He thought the case was taking a more favourable turn. For Bhavani, it was an impossibility to imagine that his son would not recover. He must live: it was his destiny to live. Bhavani was much struck with the behaviour of Sailen. It was difficult to believe that he was not of their own kith and kin. He supposed all this kindness to be due to the town training which Sailen had received. Bhavani spoke to Sailen disparagingly of the country habits which village people like himself got into.

Gradually the fever went down and Kalipada recovered consciousness. He was astonished beyond measure when he saw his father sitting in the room beside him. His first anxiety was lest he should discover the miserable state in which he had been living. But what would be harder still to bear was, if his father with his rustic manners became the butt of the people upstairs. He looked round him, but could not recognize his own room and wondered if he had been dreaming. But he found himself too weak to think.

He supposed that it had been his father who had removed him to this better lodging, but he had no power to calculate how he could possibly bear the expense. The only thing that concerned him at that moment was that he felt he must live, and for that he had a claim upon the world.

Once when his father was absent Sailen came in with a plate of grapes in his hand. Kalipada could not understand this at all and wondered if there was some practical joke behind it. He at once became excited and wondered how he could save his father from annoyance. Sailen set the plate down on the table and touched Kalipada's feet humbly and said: "My offence has been great: pray forgive me."

Kalipada started and sat up on his bed. He could see that Sailen's repentance was sincere and he was greatly moved.

When Kalipada had first come to the students' lodging house he had felt strongly drawn towards this handsome youth. He never missed a chance of looking at his face when Sailen passed by his room on his way upstairs. He would have given all the world to be friends with him, but the barrier was too great to overcome. Now to-day when Sailen brought him the grapes and asked his forgiveness, he silently looked at his face and silently accepted the grapes which spoke of his repentance.

It amused Kalipada greatly when he noticed the intimacy that had sprung up between his father and Sailen. Sailen used to call Bhavani Charan "grandfather" and exercised to the full the grandchild's privilege of joking with him. The principal object of the jokes was the absent "grandmother." Sailen made the confession that he had taken the opportunity of Kalipada's illness to steal all the delicious chutnies which his "grandmother" had made with her own hand. The news of his act of "thieving" gave Kalipada very great joy. He found it easy to deprive himself, if he could find any one who could appreciate the good things made by his mother. Thus this time of his convalescence became the happiest period in the whole of Kalipada's life.

There was only one flaw in this unalloyed happiness. Kalipada had a fierce pride in his poverty which prevented him ever speaking about his family's better days. Therefore when his father used to talk of his former prosperity Kalipada winced. Bhavani could not keep to himself the one great event of his life,—the theft of that will which he was absolutely certain that he would some day recover. Kalipada had always regarded this as a kind of mania of his father's, and in collusion with his mother he had often humoured his father concerning this amiable weakness. But he shrank in shame when his father talked about this to Sailen. He noticed particularly that Sailen did not relish such conversation and that he often tried to prove, with a certain amount of feeling, its absurdity. But Bhavani, who was ready to give in to others in matters much more serious, in this matter was adamant. Kalipada tried to pacify him by saying that there was no great need to worry about it, because those who were enjoying its benefit were almost the same as his own children, since they were his nephews.

Such talk Sailen could not bear for long and he used to leave the room. This pained Kalipada, because he thought that Sailen might get quite a wrong conception of his father and imagine him to be a grasping worldly old man. Sailen would have revealed his own relationship to Kalipada and his father long before, but this discussion about the theft of the will prevented him. It was hard for him to believe that his grandfather or father had stolen the will; on the other hand he could not but think that some cruel injustice had been done in depriving Bhavani of his share of the ancestral property. Therefore he gave up arguing when the subject was brought forward and took some occasion to leave as soon as possible.

Though Kalipada still had headaches in the evening, with a slight rise in temperature, he did not take it at all seriously. He became anxious to resume his studies because he felt it would be a calamity to him if he again missed his scholarship. He secretly began to read once more, without taking any notice of the strict orders of the doctor. Kalipada asked his father to return home, assuring him that he was in the best of health. Bhavani had been all his life fed and nourished and cooked for by his wife; he was pining to get back. He did not therefore wait to be pressed.

On the morning of his intended departure, when he went to say good-bye to Kalipada, he found him very ill indeed, his face red with fever and his whole body burning. He had been committing to memory page after page of his text book of Logic half through the night, and for the remainder he could not sleep at all. The doctor took Sailen aside. "This relapse," he said, "is fatal." Sailen came to Bhavani and said, "The patient requires a mother's nursing: she must be brought to Calcutta."

It was evening when Rashmani came, and she only saw her son alive for a few hours. Not knowing how her husband could survive such a terrible shock she altogether suppressed her own sorrow. Her son was merged in her husband again, and she took up this burden of the dead and the living on her own aching heart. She said to her God,—"It is too much for me to bear." But she did bear it.

V

It was midnight. With the very weariness of her sorrow Rashmani had fallen asleep soon after reaching her own home in the village. But Bhavani had no sleep that night. Tossing on his bed for hours he heaved a deep sigh saying,—"Merciful God!" Then he got up from his bed and went out. He entered the room where Kalipada had been wont to do his lessons in his childhood. The lamp shook as he held it in his hand. On the wooden settle there was still the torn, ink-stained quilt, made long ago by Rashmani herself. On the wall were figures of Euclid and Algebra drawn in charcoal. The remains of a Royal Reader No. III and a few exercise books were lying about; and the one odd slipper of his infancy, which had evaded notice so long, was keeping its place in the dusty obscurity of the corner of the room. To-day it had become so important that nothing in the world, however great, could keep it hidden any longer. Bhavani put the lamp in the niche on the wall and silently sat on the settle; his eyes were dry, but he felt choked as if with want of breath.

Bhavani opened the shutters on the eastern side and stood still, grasping the iron bars, gazing into the darkness. Through the drizzling rain he could see the outline of the clump of trees at the end of the outer wall. At this spot Kalipada had made his own garden. The passion flowers which he had planted with his own hand had grown densely thick. While he gazed at this Bhavani felt his heart come up into his throat with choking pain. There was nobody now to wait for and expect daily. The summer vacation had come, but no one would come back home to fill the vacant room and use its old familiar furniture.

"O Baba mine!" he cried, "O Baba! O Baba mine!"

He sat down. The rain came faster. A sound of footsteps was heard among the grass and withered leaves. Bhavani's heart stood still. He hoped it was ... that which was beyond all hope. He thought it was Kalipada himself come to see his own garden,—and in this downpour of rain how wet he would be! Anxiety about this made him restless. Then somebody stood for a moment in front of the iron window bars. The cloak round his head made it impossible for Bhavani to see his face clearly, but his height was the same as that of Kalipada.

"Darling!" cried Bhavani, "You have come!" and he rushed to open the door.

But when he came outside to the spot where the figure had stood, there was no one to be seen. He walked up and down in the garden through the drenching rain, but no one was there. He stood still for a moment raising his voice and calling,—"Kalipada," but no answer came. The servant, Noto, who was sleeping in the cowshed, heard his cry and came out and coaxed him back to his room.

Next day, in the morning, Noto, while sweeping the room found a bundle just underneath the grated window. He brought it to Bhavani who opened it and found it was an old document. He put on his spectacles and after reading a few lines came rushing in to Rashmani and gave the paper into her hand.

Rashmani asked, "What is it?"

Bhavani replied, "It is the will!"

"Who gave it you?"

"He himself came last night to give it to me."

"What are you going to do with it?"

Bhavani said: "I have no need of it now." And he tore the will to pieces.

When the news reached the village Bagala proudly nodded his head and said: "Didn't I prophesy that the will would be recovered through Kalipada?"

But the grocer Ramcharan replied: "Last night when the ten o'clock train reached the Station a handsome looking young man came to my shop and asked the way to the Chowdhuri's house and I thought he had some kind of bundle in his hand."

"Absurd," said Bagala.

THE BABUS OF NAYANJORE

I

Once upon a time the Babus at Nayanjore were famous landholders. They were noted for their princely extravagance. They would tear off the rough border of their Dacca muslin, because it rubbed against their delicate skin. They could spend many thousands of rupees over the wedding of a kitten. And on a certain grand occasion it is alleged that in order to turn night into day they lighted numberless lamps and showered silver threads from the sky to imitate sunlight.

Those were the days before the flood. The flood came. The line of succession among these old-world Babus, with their lordly habits, could not continue for long. Like a lamp with too many wicks burning, the oil flared away quickly, and the light went out.

Kailas Babu, our neighbour, is the last relic of this extinct magnificence. Before he grew up, his family had very nearly reached its lowest ebb. When his father died, there was one dazzling outburst of funeral extravagance, and then insolvency. The property was sold to liquidate the debt. What little ready money was left over was altogether insufficient to keep up the past ancestral splendours.

Kailas Babu left Nayanjore and came to Calcutta. His son did not remain long in this world of faded glory. He died, leaving behind him an only daughter.

In Calcutta we are Kailas Babu's neighbours. Curiously enough our own family history is just the opposite of his. My father got his money by his own exertions, and prided himself on never spending a penny more than was needed. His clothes were those of a working man, and his hands also. He never had any inclination to earn the title of Babu by extravagant display; and

I myself, his only son, owe him gratitude for that. He gave me the very best education, and I was able to make my way in the world. I am not ashamed of the fact that I am a self-made man. Crisp bank-notes in my safe are dearer to me than a long pedigree in an empty family chest.

I believe this was why I disliked seeing Kailas Babu drawing his heavy cheques on the public credit from the bankrupt bank of his ancient Babu reputation. I used to fancy that he looked down on me, because my father had earned money with his own hands.

I ought to have noticed that no one showed any vexation towards Kailas Babu except myself. Indeed it would have been difficult to find an old man who did less harm than he. He was always ready with his kindly little acts of courtesy in times of sorrow and joy. He would join in all the ceremonies and religious observances of his neighbours. His familiar smile would greet young and old alike. His politeness in asking details about domestic affairs was untiring. The friends who met him in the street were perforce ready to be button-holed, while a long string of questions of this kind followed one another from his lips:

"My dear friend, I am delighted to see you. Are you quite well? How is Shashi? And Dada—is he all right? Do you know, I've only just heard that Madhu's son has got fever. How is he? Have you heard? And Hari Charan Babu—I have not seen him for a long time—I hope he is not ill. What's the matter with Rakkhal? And er—er, how are the ladies of your family?"

Kailas Babu was spotlessly neat in his dress on all occasions, though his supply of clothes was sorely limited. Every day he used to air his shirts and vests and coats and trousers carefully, and put them out in the sun, along with his bed-quilt, his pillowcase, and the small carpet on which he always sat. After airing them he would shake them, and brush them, and put them carefully away. His little bits of furniture made his small room decent, and hinted that there was more in reserve if needed. Very often, for want of a servant, he would shut up his house for a while. Then he would iron out his shirts and linen with his own hands, and do other little menial tasks. After this he would open his door and receive his friends again.

Though Kailas Babu, as I have said, had lost all his landed property, he had still some family heirlooms left. There was a silver cruet for sprinkling scented water, a filigree box for otto-of-roses, a small gold salver, a costly ancient shawl, and the old-fashioned ceremonial dress and ancestral turban. These he had rescued with the greatest difficulty from the money-lenders' clutches. On every suitable occasion he would bring them out in state, and thus try to save the world-famed dignity of the Babus of Nayanjore. At heart the most modest of men, in his daily speech he regarded it as a sacred duty, owed to his rank, to give free play to his family pride. His friends would encourage this trait in his character with kindly good-humour, and it gave them great amusement.

The neighbourhood soon learnt to call him their Thakur Dada. They would flock to his house and sit with him for hours together. To prevent his incurring any expense, one or other of his friends would bring him tobacco and say: "Thakur Dada, this morning some tobacco was sent to me from Gaya. Do take it and see how you like it."

Thakur Dada would take it and say it was excellent. He would then go on to tell of a certain exquisite tobacco which they once smoked in the old days of Nayanjore at the cost of a guinea an ounce.

"I wonder," he used to say, "if any one would like to try it now. I have some left, and can get it at once."

Every one knew that, if they asked for it, then somehow or other the key of the cupboard would be missing; or else Ganesh, his old family servant, had put it away somewhere.

"You never can be sure," he would add, "where things go to when servants are about. Now, this Ganesh of mine,—I can't tell you what a fool he is, but I haven't the heart to dismiss him."

Ganesh, for the credit of the family, was quite ready to bear all the blame without a word.

One of the company usually said at this point: "Never mind, Thakur Dada. Please don't trouble to look for it. This tobacco we're smoking will do quite well. The other would be too strong."

Then Thakur Dada would be relieved and settle down again, and the talk would go on.

When his guests got up to go away, Thakur Dada would accompany them to the door and say to them on the door-step: "Oh, by the way, when are you all coming to dine with me?"

One or other of us would answer: "Not just yet, Thakur Dada, not just yet. We'll fix a day later."

"Quite right," he would answer. "Quite right. We had much better wait till the rains come. It's too hot now. And a grand rich dinner such as I should want to give you would upset us in weather like this."

But when the rains did come, every one was very careful not to remind him of his promise. If the subject was brought up, some friend would suggest gently that it was very inconvenient to get about when the rains were so severe, and therefore it would be much better to wait till they were over. Thus the game went on.

Thakur Dada's poor lodging was much too small for his position, and we used to condole with him about it. His friends would assure him they quite understood his difficulties: it was next to impossible to get a decent house in Calcutta. Indeed, they had all been looking out for years for a house to suit him. But, I need hardly add, no friend had been foolish enough to find one. Thakur Dada used to say, with a sigh of resignation: "Well, well, I suppose I shall have to put up with this house after all." Then he would add with a genial smile: "But, you know, I could never bear to be away from my friends. I must be near you. That really compensates for everything."

Somehow I felt all this very deeply indeed. I suppose the real reason was, that when a man is young, stupidity appears to him the worst of crimes. Kailas Babu was not really stupid. In ordinary business matters every one was ready to consult him. But with regard to Nayanjore his utterances were certainly void of common sense. Because, out of amused affection for him, no one contradicted his impossible statements, he refused to keep them in bounds. When people recounted in his hearing the glorious history of Nayanjore with absurd exaggerations, he would accept all they said with the utmost gravity, and never doubted, even in his dreams, that any one could disbelieve it.

II

When I sit down and try to analyse the thoughts and feelings that I had towards Kailas Babu, I see that there was a still deeper reason for my dislike. I will now explain.

Though I am the son of a rich man, and might have wasted time at college, my industry was such that I took my M.A. degree in Calcutta University when quite young. My moral character was flawless. In addition, my outward appearance was so handsome, that if I were to call myself beautiful, it might be thought a mark of self-estimation, but could not be considered an untruth.

There could be no question that among the young men of Bengal I was regarded by parents generally as a very eligible match. I was myself quite clear on the point and had determined to obtain my full value in the marriage market. When I pictured my choice, I had before my mind's eye a wealthy father's only daughter, extremely beautiful and highly educated. Proposals came pouring in to me from far and near; large sums in cash were offered. I weighed these offers with rigid impartiality in the delicate scales of my own estimation. But there was no one fit to be my partner. I became convinced, with the poet Bhabavuti, that,

In this world's endless time and boundless space

One may be born at last to match my sovereign grace.

But in this puny modern age, and this contracted space of modern Bengal, it was doubtful if the peerless creature existed as yet.

Meanwhile my praises were sung in many tunes, and in different metres, by designing parents.

Whether I was pleased with their daughters or not, this worship which they offered was never unpleasing. I used to regard it as my proper due, because I was so good. We are told that when the gods withhold their boons from mortals they still expect their worshippers to pay them fervent honour and are angry if it is withheld. I had that divine expectance strongly developed in myself.

I have already mentioned that Thakur Dada had an only grand-daughter. I had seen her many times, but had never mistaken her for beautiful. No thought had ever entered my mind that she would be a possible partner for myself. All the same, it seemed quite certain to me that some day or other Kailas Babu would offer her, with all due worship, as an oblation at my shrine. Indeed—this was the inner secret of my dislike—I was thoroughly annoyed that he had not done so already.

I heard that Thakur Dada had told his friends that the Babus of Nayanjore never craved a boon. Even if the girl remained unmarried, he would not break the family tradition. It was this arrogance of his that made me angry. My indignation smouldered for some time. But I remained perfectly silent and bore it with the utmost patience, because I was so good.

As lightning accompanies thunder, so in my character a flash of humour was mingled with the mutterings of my wrath. It was, of course, impossible for me to punish the old man merely to give vent to my rage; and for a long time I did nothing at all. But suddenly one day such an amusing plan came into my head, that I could not resist the temptation of carrying it into effect.

I have already said that many of Kailas Babu's friends used to flatter the old man's vanity to the full. One, who was a retired Government servant, had told him that whenever he saw the Chota Lât Sahib he always asked for the latest news about the Babus of Nayanjore, and the Chota Lât had been heard to say that in all Bengal the only really respectable families were those of the Maharaja of Cossipore and the Babus of Nayanjore. When this monstrous falsehood was told to Kailas Babu he was extremely gratified and often repeated the story. And wherever after that he met this Government servant in company he would ask, along with other questions:

"Oh! er—by the way, how is the Chota Lât Sahib? Quite well, did you say? Ah, yes, I am so delighted to hear it! And the dear Mem Sahib, is she quite well too? Ah, yes! and the little children—are they quite well also? Ah, yes!

that's very good news! Be sure and give them my compliments when you see them."

Kailas Babu would constantly express his intention of going some day and paying a visit to the Lord Sahib. But it may be taken for granted that many Chota Lâts and Burra Lâts also would come and go, and much water would pass down the Hoogly, before the family coach of Nayanjore would be furbished up to pay a visit to Government House.

One day I took Kailas Babu aside and told him in a whisper: "Thakur Dada, I was at the Levee yesterday, and the Chota Lât Sahib happened to mention the Babus of Nayanjore. I told him that Kailas Babu had come to town. Do you know, he was terribly hurt because you hadn't called. He told me he was going to put etiquette on one side and pay you a private visit himself this very afternoon."

Anybody else could have seen through this plot of mine in a moment. And, if it had been directed against another person, Kailas Babu would have understood the joke. But after all that he had heard from his friend the Government servant, and after all his own exaggerations, a visit from the Lieutenant-Governor seemed the most natural thing in the world. He became highly nervous and excited at my news. Each detail of the coming visit exercised him greatly,—most of all his own ignorance of English. How on earth was that difficulty to be met? I told him there was no difficulty at all: it was aristocratic not to know English: and, besides, the Lieutenant-Governor always brought an interpreter with him, and he had expressly mentioned that this visit was to be private.

About midday, when most of our neighbours are at work, and the rest are asleep, a carriage and pair stopped before the lodging of Kailas Babu. Two flunkeys in livery came up the stairs, and announced in a loud voice, "The Chota Lât Sahib has arrived!" Kailas Babu was ready, waiting for him, in his old-fashioned ceremonial robes and ancestral turban, and Ganesh was by his side, dressed in his master's best suit of clothes for the occasion.

When the Chota Lât Sahib was announced, Kailas Babu ran panting and puffing and trembling to the door, and led in a friend of mine, in disguise, with repeated salaams, bowing low at each step and walking backward as best he could. He had his old family shawl spread over a hard wooden chair and he asked the Lât Sahib to be seated. He then made a high-flown speech in Urdu, the ancient Court language of the Sahibs, and presented on the golden salver a string of gold mohurs, the last relics of his broken fortune. The old family servant Ganesh, with an expression of awe bordering on terror, stood behind with the scent-sprinkler, drenching the Lât Sahib, and touched him gingerly from time to time with the otto-of-roses from the filigree box.

Kailas Babu repeatedly expressed his regret at not being able to receive His Honour Bahadur with all the ancestral magnificence of his own family estate at Nayanjore. There he could have welcomed him properly with due ceremonial. But in Calcutta he was a mere stranger and sojourner,—in fact a fish out of water.

My friend, with his tall silk hat on, very gravely nodded. I need hardly say that according to English custom the hat ought to have been removed inside the room. But my friend did not dare to take it off for fear of detection: and Kailas Babu and his old servant Ganesh were sublimely unconscious of the breach of etiquette.

After a ten minutes' interview, which consisted chiefly of nodding the head, my friend rose to his feet to depart. The two flunkeys in livery, as had been planned beforehand, carried off in state the string of gold mohurs, the gold salver, the old ancestral shawl, the silver scent-sprinkler, and the otto-of-roses filigree box; they placed them ceremoniously in the carriage. Kailas Babu regarded this as the usual habit of Chota Lât Sahibs.

I was watching all the while from the next room. My sides were aching with suppressed laughter. When I could hold myself in no longer, I rushed into a further room, suddenly to discover, in a corner, a young girl sobbing as if her heart would break. When she saw my uproarious laughter she stood upright in passion, flashing the lightning of her big dark eyes in mine, and said with a tear-choked voice: "Tell me! What harm has my grandfather done to you? Why have you come to deceive him? Why have you come here? Why——"

She could say no more. She covered her face with her hands and broke into sobs.

My laughter vanished in a moment. It had never occurred to me that there was anything but a supremely funny joke in this act of mine, and here I discovered that I had given the cruellest pain to this tenderest little heart. All the ugliness of my cruelty rose up to condemn me. I slunk out of the room in silence, like a kicked dog.

Hitherto I had only looked upon Kusum, the grand-daughter of Kailas Babu, as a somewhat worthless commodity in the marriage market, waiting in vain to attract a husband. But now I found, with a shock of surprise, that in the corner of that room a human heart was beating.

The whole night through I had very little sleep. My mind was in a tumult. On the next day, very early in the morning, I took all those stolen goods back to Kailas Babu's lodgings, wishing to hand them over in secret to the servant Ganesh. I waited outside the door, and, not finding any one, went upstairs to Kailas Babu's room. I heard from the passage Kusum asking her grandfather in the most winning voice: "Dada, dearest, do tell me all that the Chota Lât Sahib said to you yesterday. Don't leave out a single word. I am dying to hear it all over again."

And Dada needed no encouragement. His face beamed over with pride as he related all manner of praises which the Lât Sahib had been good enough to utter concerning the ancient families of Nayanjore. The girl was seated before him, looking up into his face, and listening with rapt attention. She was determined, out of love for the old man, to play her part to the full.

My heart was deeply touched, and tears came to my eyes. I stood there in silence in the passage, while Thakur Dada finished all his embellishments of the Chota Lât Sahib's wonderful visit. When he left the room at last, I took the stolen goods and laid them at the feet of the girl and came away without a word.

Later in the day I called again to see Kailas Babu himself. According to our ugly modern custom, I had been in the habit of making no greeting at all to this old man when I came into the room. But on this day I made a low bow and touched his feet. I am convinced the old man thought that the coming of the Chota Lât Sahib to his house was the cause of my new politeness. He was highly gratified by it, and an air of benign serenity shone from his eyes. His friends had looked in, and he had already begun to tell again at full length the story of the Lieutenant-Governor's visit with still further adornments of a most fantastic kind. The interview was already becoming an epic, both in quality and in length.

When the other visitors had taken their leave, I made my proposal to the old man in a humble manner. I told him that, "though I could never for a moment hope to be worthy of marriage connection with such an illustrious family, yet ... etc. etc."

When I made clear my proposal of marriage, the old man embraced me and broke out in a tumult of joy: "I am a poor man, and could never have expected such great good fortune."

That was the first and last time in his life that Kailas Babu confessed to being poor. It was also the first and last time in his life that he forgot, if only for a single moment, the ancestral dignity that belongs to the Babus of Nayanjore.

●